Updated Bermuda Travel Guide

Ruby Shawn

Updated Bermuda Travel Guide

A Comprehensive Guide to Explore the Rich History, iconic tourist spots, Natural Wonders, Vibrant Culture, and Stunning Landscapes of Bermuda and Travel Tips from Locals

By

Ruby Shawn

Copyright

© **Ruby Shawn**, 2023

All rights reserved. No part of this book may be reproduced, stored in a retrieval system, or transmitted, in any form or by any means, without the prior written permission of the copyright owner, except in the case of brief quotations embodied in critical reviews and certain other noncommercial uses permitted by copyright law.

Disclaimer:

The information provided in this book, "Updated Bermuda Travel Guide," is for general informational purposes only. While every effort has been made to ensure the accuracy and timeliness of the information presented, the author and publisher make no representations or warranties of any kind, express or implied, about the completeness, accuracy, reliability, suitability, or availability with respect to the book or the information, products, services, or related graphics contained within it.

The use of the information provided in this book is at the reader's own risk. The author and publisher shall not be liable for any loss or damage, including but not limited to indirect or consequential loss or damage, arising from the use of the information in this book.

It is recommended that readers independently verify any information provided in this book and make their own decisions based on their personal judgment and discretion.

Updated Bermuda Travel Guide

Ruby Shawn

Table of Content

Table of Content 5
Introduction to Bermuda 8
   History and Culture 11
   Geography and Climate 14
   Getting to Bermuda 16
      Practical Tips 19
Exploring Bermuda's Regions 20
   Hamilton Parish 23
   St. George's Parish 25
   Smith's Parish 27
   Devonshire Parish 29
   Pembroke Parish 31
   Paget Parish 33
   Warwick Parish 36
   Southampton Parish 38
   Sandys Parish 40
   Other Islands in Bermuda 42
Top Attractions in Bermuda 46
   Horseshoe Bay Beach 48
   Royal Naval Dockyard 50
   St. Peter's Church 52
   Bermuda Aquarium, Museum & Zoo 54
   Crystal Caves 56
   Gibbs Hill Lighthouse 58

Bermuda Underwater Exploration Institute 60
Spittal Pond Nature Reserve 62
Botanical Gardens 64
Historical Sites and Museums 66
Outdoor Activities and Adventures 70
Water Sports and Beaches 72
Snorkeling and Diving 74
Sailing and Boating 76
Golfing in Bermuda 78
Hiking and Nature Trails 80
Fishing and Deep-Sea Excursions 82
Cave Explorations 84
Whale Watching 86
Eco-Tourism in Bermuda 88
Festivals and Events 90
Dining and Cuisine in Bermuda 92
Traditional Bermudian Cuisine 94
Seafood Specialties 96
International and Fusion Cuisine 98
Local Food Markets and Restaurants 100
Fine Dining Experiences 102
Street Food and Casual Eateries 104
Afternoon Tea and Cocktails 106
Bermudian Rum and Beer 108
Shopping and Souvenirs 110
Bermuda's Shopping Districts 112
Local Art and Handicrafts 114

Ruby Shawn

Traditional Clothing and Textiles 116
Jewelry and Precious Gems 118
Duty-Free Shopping 120
Souvenir Ideas and Recommendations 122
Practical Travel Tips 124
Accommodation Options 126
Transportation within Bermuda 128
Currency and Banking 130
Language and Communication 132
Health and Safety 134
Customs and Etiquette 136
Tipping and Service Charges 138
Travel Insurance and Documentation 140
Useful Phrases and Vocabulary 142
Sustainable Tourism Practices 144
Conclusion 147

INTRODUCTION TO BERMUDA

Welcome to Bermuda, a captivating island paradise nestled in the Atlantic Ocean. With its pink sandy beaches, turquoise waters, and charming pastel-colored houses, Bermuda is a destination that truly enchants every visitor. This guide is your key to unlocking the wonders of this unique and vibrant island.

Bermuda, a British Overseas Territory, is located approximately 650 miles off the coast of North Carolina. Despite its name, Bermuda is not a single island but an archipelago consisting of 181 islands and islets. Bridges and causeways connect the main islands. The largest of these islands is connected by a 21-mile stretch of road known as the South Shore Road.

The history of Bermuda is rich and diverse, dating back to its discovery by Spanish explorer Juan de Bermúdez in 1505. The English settled the island in 1609, when the ship Sea Venture en route to Jamestown, Virginia, was shipwrecked on its treacherous reefs. This historical event gave rise to the legend of Bermuda's infamous "Triangle."

Today, Bermuda is renowned for its pristine beaches, which boast unique pink sand derived from the shells and skeletons of marine organisms called foraminifera. Horseshoe Bay Beach, with its crescent-shaped shore and crystal-clear waters, is a must-visit destination for sun-seekers and nature enthusiasts. Other notable beaches include Elbow Beach, Warwick Long Bay, and Tobacco Bay, each offering its own distinct beauty.

Beyond its natural wonders, Bermuda is home to a wealth of cultural treasures. Explore the UNESCO World Heritage Site of St. George's, a charming town founded in 1612 and filled with picturesque architecture, cobblestone streets, and historical landmarks. Discover the maritime heritage of the island at the Royal Naval Dockyard, a former British naval base that now houses museums, shops, and art galleries.

For those seeking adventure, Bermuda offers a plethora of outdoor activities. Dive into the mesmerizing underwater world through snorkeling or scuba diving excursions, where you can explore vibrant coral reefs teeming with colorful marine life. Set sail on a catamaran or charter a boat to discover hidden coves, secluded beaches, and even shipwrecks. Golf enthusiasts can tee off on world-class golf courses with breathtaking ocean views.

No trip to Bermuda is complete without indulging in its delectable cuisine. Savour traditional Bermudian dishes like fish chowder, cassava pie, and shark hash. Explore the island's thriving culinary scene, which blends international flavors with local ingredients. From fine dining establishments to casual beachside eateries, Bermuda offers a diverse range of culinary experiences to satisfy every palate.

As you embark on your journey through Bermuda, this travel guide will serve as your trusty companion, providing invaluable information on the island's regions, top attractions, outdoor adventures, dining options, shopping delights, and practical travel tips. Whether you're a first-time visitor or a seasoned traveler, Bermuda promises a captivating experience that will leave you with cherished memories.

So, pack your swimsuit, grab your camera, and get ready to immerse yourself in the beauty, history, and warmth of Bermuda. Let this travel guide be your gateway to discovering this idyllic island paradise's hidden gems and enchanting secrets. Welcome to Bermuda, where paradise meets adventure!

History and Culture

The history and culture of Bermuda are as fascinating and diverse as the island itself. From its early colonization to its unique blend of influences, Bermuda's rich heritage has shaped its identity over the centuries.

Bermuda's history dates back to the early 17th century when the English settled the island. The arrival of the Sea Venture shipwrecked on the Bermuda reefs in 1609 marked the beginning of the permanent settlement. The survivors of the shipwreck, including Admiral Sir George Somers, established a new colony on the island. This event also gave rise to the popular legend of the Bermuda Triangle.

During the 17th and 18th centuries, Bermuda thrived as a center for shipbuilding and maritime trade. Its strategic location in the Atlantic Ocean made it a vital outpost for the British Empire. The island served as a naval base during both World Wars and remnants of its military past can still be seen today in places like the Royal Naval Dockyard.

The cultural heritage of Bermuda is a vibrant mix of African, British, Caribbean, and American influences. The descendants of enslaved Africans brought to Bermuda have made significant contributions to the island's culture, music, and traditions. Gombey dancing, a traditional African-inspired dance with colorful costumes, rhythmic drumming, and lively movements, is an important part of Bermuda's cultural landscape.

Bermuda's architecture is characterized by its charming pastel-colored houses with white roofs. This distinctive style is rooted in the island's history as a British colony. The roofs were initially painted white to collect rainwater, which was stored in tanks for drinking water. Today, these roofs have become an iconic symbol of Bermuda's architectural heritage.

Bermuda's cultural calendar is filled with vibrant festivals and events. The Bermuda Day Parade, held on the last Friday in May, showcases the island's heritage through music, dance, and colorful floats. The Bermuda Festival of the Performing Arts brings together local and international artists for a month-long celebration of music, theater, and dance. The Cup Match, a two-day cricket match held in August, is a beloved tradition that celebrates Bermuda's Emancipation Day.

The cuisine of Bermuda reflects its diverse cultural influences. Traditional Bermudian dishes often feature fresh seafood, including fish such as wahoo, rockfish, and spiny lobster. Local favorites include fish chowder, codfish and potatoes, and shark hash. Bermuda's culinary scene has also embraced international flavors, offering a wide range of dining options, from casual beachside eateries to fine dining restaurants.

Bermuda's cultural heritage is also preserved and celebrated through its museums and historical sites. The National Museum of Bermuda showcases the island's maritime history, while the Bermuda Underwater Exploration Institute takes visitors on a journey through the depths of the ocean. St. George's, a UNESCO World Heritage Site, offers a glimpse into Bermuda's colonial past with its well-preserved architecture and historical landmarks.

As you explore Bermuda, take the time to immerse yourself in its captivating history and vibrant culture. From the island's early colonization to its unique blend of traditions and influences, Bermuda's past and present come together to create an enriching and unforgettable experience.

Geography and Climate

Nestled in the vast expanse of the Atlantic Ocean, Bermuda is an archipelago of 181 islands and islets located approximately 650 miles off the east coast of the United States. Despite its name, Bermuda is not located in the Caribbean but is considered part of the North Atlantic region.

The geography of Bermuda is defined by its main islands, which are connected by bridges and causeways. The largest of these islands is connected by a 21-mile stretch of road known as the South Shore Road. The total land area of Bermuda is approximately 21 square miles, making it one of the world's smallest inhabited territories.

One of the most striking features of Bermuda's geography is its stunning coastline. The island is surrounded by a network of coral reefs, which provide protection from the open ocean and create calm, clear turquoise waters. These reefs also make Bermuda a popular destination for snorkeling and scuba diving, allowing visitors to explore vibrant coral formations and a diverse array of marine life.

Bermuda's beaches are renowned for their pink sand, which is a result of the pulverized red shells and coral that mix with the white sand. Horseshoe Bay Beach, with its pink sand and crescent-shaped shoreline, is a true gem and one of the most iconic beaches on the island. Other notable beaches include Elbow Beach, Warwick Long Bay, and Tobacco Bay, each offering its own unique beauty and charm.

The climate of Bermuda is classified as subtropical, characterized by mild winters and warm summers. The island's pleasant year-round climate makes it an ideal destination for outdoor activities and beach relaxation. The average temperature in Bermuda ranges from the low 70s Fahrenheit (around 22°C) in the winter to the mid-80s Fahrenheit (around 30°C) in the summer.

Bermuda's unique location in the Atlantic Ocean exposes it to the influence of both tropical and temperate weather systems. The hurricane season, which typically runs from June to November, poses a potential risk. However, Bermuda's building codes and infrastructure are designed to withstand these storms. It's always advisable to stay informed about weather conditions and any potential tropical disturbances before planning a trip to Bermuda.

In addition to its beautiful beaches and clear waters, Bermuda boasts a lush and picturesque landscape. The island is dotted with gardens and nature reserves, showcasing a variety of flora and fauna. The Bermuda Botanical Gardens, for instance, offer a tranquil oasis with a vast array of tropical plants. At the same time, the Spittal Pond Nature Reserve provides opportunities for bird-watching and scenic walks.

Whether you're strolling along pink sandy beaches, exploring underwater worlds, or taking in the island's scenic beauty, Bermuda's geography and climate create an idyllic backdrop for a truly memorable experience.

Getting to Bermuda

Bermuda, a captivating island paradise in the Atlantic Ocean, is a sought-after destination for travelers seeking stunning beaches, vibrant culture, and a relaxing getaway. Despite its remote location, getting to Bermuda is relatively convenient thanks to its well-connected transportation options.

By Air

The primary gateway to Bermuda is L.F. Wade International Airport (BDA), located in St. George's Parish. The airport serves as a hub for both international and regional flights. Numerous major airlines operate regular flights to Bermuda from various cities in the United States, Canada, and the United Kingdom. Direct flights are available from major hubs such as New York, Miami, Atlanta, Toronto, and London. Flight durations vary depending on the origin, ranging from around 2 to 8 hours.

By Sea

Another popular way to reach Bermuda is by cruise ship. Several major cruise lines offer itineraries that include Bermuda as a port of call. Cruise ships dock at the Royal Naval Dockyard, located on the island's western end. This gives passengers the opportunity to explore Bermuda's attractions and experience its beauty during their stay. The cruise season typically runs from April to October.

Visa Requirements

Before planning your trip to Bermuda, checking the visa requirements is essential. Visitors from many countries, including the United States, Canada, the United Kingdom, and the European Union, do not need a visa for short stays in Bermuda. However, it is advisable to ensure that your passport has a validity of at least six months beyond your planned departure date. It is also crucial to check if you require any specific travel documentation based on your nationality.

Transportation within Bermuda

Once you arrive in Bermuda, getting around the island is convenient and enjoyable. The main mode of transportation is by taxi or minibus. Taxis are readily available at the airport and other popular locations, and they operate on a metered system. Minibusses are a more economical option and follow designated routes around the island.

Bermuda's public transportation system also includes a reliable bus network. Buses are a great way to explore the island and reach various destinations, including beaches, shopping districts, and historical sites. Bus routes cover the main regions of Bermuda, and fares are reasonable.

For those who prefer more independent exploration, renting a scooter or bicycle is a popular choice. Bermuda has well-maintained roads, and scooters are a common sight on the island. However, it's important to note that driving is on the left-hand side, and visitors are required to obtain a temporary driving permit, which can be obtained from rental agencies or the Transport Control Department.

Practical Tips

When planning your trip to Bermuda, it's advisable to consider a few practical tips. As Bermuda is a popular destination, especially during peak tourist seasons, booking your flights and accommodations well in advance is recommended to secure the best options and prices.

Additionally, packing essentials such as lightweight clothing, swimwear, sunscreen, and comfortable walking shoes are essential. Bermuda's subtropical climate means that the weather is generally warm throughout the year, but it's advisable to check the forecast and pack accordingly.

Lastly, it's always a good idea to have travel insurance that covers medical emergencies, trip cancellations, and lost luggage. Familiarize yourself with any COVID-19-related travel requirements and restrictions that may be in place during your visit.

As you plan your journey to Bermuda, the ease of access and convenient transportation options ensure that your arrival and exploration of this idyllic island are as enjoyable as the destination itself. Get ready to experience the magic of Bermuda and create memories that will last a lifetime.

EXPLORING BERMUDA'S REGIONS

As you embark on your journey through Bermuda, get ready to discover the diverse and enchanting regions that make up this captivating island paradise. From the historic charm of St. George's to the vibrant energy of Hamilton, each region of Bermuda has its own unique character and attractions to explore.

St. George's, a UNESCO World Heritage Site, is the oldest and most picturesque town on the island. Its cobblestone streets, pastel-colored buildings, and historic landmarks transport you back in time. Explore Fort St. Catherine, visit the Tucker House Museum, or simply wander through the town's narrow alleys to soak up its rich history and colonial charm.

Hamilton, the capital of Bermuda, offers a lively blend of modernity and tradition. This bustling city is the island's commercial hub, featuring various shops, restaurants, and cultural attractions. From the elegant Victorian-style buildings along Front Street to the vibrant markets of the City of Hamilton, there is always something to discover in this vibrant region.

The Royal Naval Dockyard, located at the western end of Bermuda, is a must-visit destination for history buffs and art enthusiasts alike. Explore the island's maritime history at the National Museum of Bermuda, stroll through the picturesque grounds of the Dockyard, or browse the numerous shops and galleries that now occupy its historic buildings.

Bermuda's South Shore is renowned for its stunning beaches, pink sand, and crystal-clear waters. From the famous Horseshoe Bay Beach to the hidden gems of Warwick Long Bay and Jobson's Cove, the South Shore offers a paradise-like experience with its pristine coastline and picturesque landscapes.

Beyond these main regions, Bermuda is dotted with charming villages, nature reserves, and hidden coves waiting to be discovered. Whether you're seeking outdoor adventures, cultural experiences, or simply relaxing on the beach, Bermuda's regions offer a wealth of possibilities to cater to every traveler's interests.

In this chapter, I will delve into each region of Bermuda, providing insights into its unique attractions, dining options, outdoor activities, and more. From the historical wonders of St. George's to the vibrant streets of Hamilton and the natural beauty of the South Shore, prepare to embark on an unforgettable exploration of Bermuda's regions and unlock the secrets of this idyllic island paradise.

Hamilton Parish

Hamilton Parish, located in the northeastern part of Bermuda, is a captivating region known for its natural beauty, historic landmarks, and vibrant cultural scene. Named after Sir Henry Hamilton, the Governor of Bermuda in the late 18th century, this Parish offers a diverse range of attractions and experiences for visitors to enjoy.

One of the highlights of Hamilton Parish is the Crystal Caves, an underground wonder that captivates with its stunning stalactites and crystal-clear pools. Descend into these majestic caves to witness nature's masterpieces and learn about their formation through guided tours. The adjacent Fantasy Cave adds to the allure, offering an enchanting experience as you explore its magical formations.

Cooper's Island Nature Reserve is another gem in Hamilton Parish. This beautiful reserve boasts pristine beaches, coastal trails, and diverse wildlife. Take a leisurely stroll along the scenic trails, spot migratory birds, and enjoy breathtaking views of the Atlantic Ocean. The reserve also has excellent snorkeling spots, allowing you to discover the vibrant marine life that inhabits the surrounding waters.

Tom Moore's Jungle, a picturesque woodland area, is a must-visit attraction in Hamilton Parish. Named after the famous Irish poet, this lush oasis offers serene walking trails amidst exotic flora and fauna. Immerse yourself in the tranquility of nature as you follow the paths that wind through the dense foliage, past charming waterfalls, and secluded pools.

History enthusiasts will be delighted by the wealth of historical landmarks in Hamilton Parish. The Unfinished Church, a hauntingly beautiful structure, stands as a testament to Bermuda's architectural heritage. Originally intended to be a replacement for St. Peter's Church, it remains a captivating site to explore. The Carter House, a restored 17th-century homestead, provides insight into the island's colonial past and showcases traditional Bermudian architecture.

Flatts Village, a charming waterfront community, offers a blend of history, art, and culinary delights. Visit the Bermuda Aquarium, Museum & Zoo, which houses a fascinating array of marine life, and explore the nearby art galleries and boutique shops. Indulge in a meal at one of the waterfront restaurants, where you can savor fresh seafood while enjoying panoramic views of the tranquil waters.

Hamilton Parish also hosts various cultural events and festivals throughout the year. The Bermuda Agricultural Exhibition, held annually in April, showcases the island's agricultural heritage with livestock shows, traditional food stalls, and local crafts. The annual Cup Match Classic, a two-day cricket match held in August, brings the community together in a celebration of sports and culture.

Hamilton Parish invites visitors to immerse themselves in the rich tapestry of Bermuda. Whether you're exploring the underground wonders of Crystal Caves, immersing yourself in nature at Cooper's Island, or delving into history at the Unfinished Church, Hamilton Parish offers a memorable and enriching experience for every traveler.

St. George's Parish

St. George's Parish, located on the northeastern tip of Bermuda, is a captivating region steeped in history and charm. As the oldest continuously inhabited English settlement in the New World, this UNESCO World Heritage Site offers a glimpse into Bermuda's colonial past and showcases its unique cultural heritage.

The town of St. George's, the main hub of the Parish, exudes a captivating atmosphere with its narrow cobblestone streets, pastel-colored buildings, and historic landmarks. The town's rich history comes to life as you explore its well-preserved architecture and visit sites like St. Peter's Church, the oldest Anglican church in the Western Hemisphere. Wander through King's Square, the heart of St. George's, and soak in the ambiance of this charming colonial town.

Fort St. Catherine, a formidable fortress dating back to the early 17th century, stands as a testament to Bermuda's strategic importance during colonial times. Explore its tunnels, ramparts, and exhibits to gain insights into Bermuda's military past and enjoy panoramic views of the surrounding coastline.

St. George's Parish's historic homes and museums provide further opportunities to delve into Bermuda's heritage. The Tucker House Museum, once the residence of Bermuda's wealthiest family, offers a glimpse into 18th-century life with its collection of antique furniture and artifacts. The Bermuda National Trust Museum at the Globe Hotel provides a comprehensive overview of Bermuda's history and culture.

Bermuda's first capital, St. George's, also serves as a cultural center with various events and festivals throughout the year. The St. George's Foundation hosts the annual Bermuda Day Parade, a vibrant celebration of the island's heritage featuring colorful floats, music, and dance performances. The St. George's Marine Expo showcases the island's maritime traditions with boat races, fishing tournaments, and nautical demonstrations.

For outdoor enthusiasts, St. George's Parish offers a range of natural attractions. Explore the trails of Cooper's Island Nature Reserve, which encompasses diverse ecosystems, scenic coastal views, and secluded beaches. Uncover the hidden beauty of Alexandra Battery Park. In this tranquil waterfront park, you can enjoy picnics, fishing, and panoramic vistas of the Atlantic Ocean.

Culinary delights await in St. George's Parish, with various restaurants and cafes offering a taste of Bermudian cuisine. Indulge in fresh seafood, traditional dishes like fish chowder and codfish and potatoes, and sample local treats such as Bermuda fish cakes and spiny lobster.

St. George's Parish is a captivating destination that invites visitors to step back in time and immerse themselves in Bermuda's rich heritage. Explore its cobblestone streets, visit its museums and forts, and soak up the enchanting ambiance of this UNESCO World Heritage Site for an unforgettable experience in Bermuda.

Smith's Parish

Smith's Parish, nestled in the central part of Bermuda, is a picturesque region that offers a delightful blend of natural beauty, historic sites, and recreational activities. Named after Sir Thomas Smith, an early settler in Bermuda, this Parish invites visitors to explore its scenic landscapes and immerse themselves in its rich heritage.

One of the highlights of Smith's Parish is John Smith's Bay, a stunning beach known for its pink sand and crystal-clear waters. This tranquil and secluded spot is perfect for sunbathing, swimming, and snorkeling. The beach is bordered by lush vegetation, creating a serene and idyllic setting for a day of relaxation.

Spittal Pond Nature Reserve is a must-visit destination for those seeking outdoor adventures. This expansive reserve is a haven for bird-watching enthusiasts, with various bird species, including herons, egrets, and cormorants. The reserve also features picturesque walking trails that wind through diverse ecosystems, including mangroves, woodlands, and wetlands. Keep an eye out for native flora and fauna as you explore this natural oasis.

For a taste of Bermuda's cultural heritage, pay a visit to the Verdmont Historic House and Gardens. This beautifully preserved 18th-century mansion showcases Bermuda's architectural style and offers a glimpse into the island's colonial past. Explore the elegant rooms, admire the antique furniture, and stroll through the meticulously maintained gardens for a step back in time.

Spice up your visit to Smith's Parish with a trip to the Bermuda Perfumery. This boutique perfumery is located in historic Stewart Hall and offers a unique olfactory experience. Discover the art of perfumery through guided tours, learn about the process of creating signature scents, and sample a range of exquisite fragrances inspired by Bermuda's natural surroundings.

Smith's Parish is also home to a range of recreational activities. Pay a visit to the Mid Ocean Club, one of the island's premier golf courses, and tee off amidst stunning ocean views and lush landscapes. Tennis enthusiasts can enjoy a game or two at the Bermuda National Tennis Stadium, which hosts international tournaments and offers top-notch facilities.

Culinary delights await in Smith's Parish, with various restaurants and eateries to satisfy every palate. Sample Bermuda's seafood specialties, such as fish sandwiches, fresh lobster, and succulent rockfish. Don't forget to try the traditional fish chowder, a spicy and flavorful dish that is a staple of Bermudian cuisine.

With its beautiful beaches, natural reserves, historic sites, and culinary offerings, this Parish has something to offer every traveler. Whether you're seeking relaxation, adventure, or a taste of island culture, Smith's Parish promises an unforgettable experience in the enchanting landscapes of Bermuda.

Devonshire Parish

Nestled in the heart of Bermuda, Devonshire Parish is a charming region that seamlessly combines natural beauty, cultural attractions, and a vibrant community. With its tranquil gardens, historic sites, and picturesque landscapes, Devonshire Parish offers a delightful escape for visitors seeking to immerse themselves in the island's charm.

One of the highlights of Devonshire Parish is the Bermuda Botanical Gardens. Spanning 36 acres, these lush gardens showcase a stunning array of tropical plants, vibrant flowers, and serene water features. Take a leisurely stroll through the winding pathways, relax in shaded gazebos, and admire the diversity of plant life that thrives in this tranquil oasis. The gardens also house the Camden House, a grand colonial mansion that serves as the official residence of Bermuda's Premier.

A visit to the Verdmont Historic House is a must for history enthusiasts. This beautifully preserved 18th-century manor offers a glimpse into Bermuda's colonial past. As you explore the rooms filled with period furniture, artwork, and antique treasures, step back in time. The meticulously maintained gardens surrounding the house provide a serene setting for a leisurely stroll.

Nature lovers will find solace in Devonshire Parish's Devonshire Bay. This secluded and pristine beach offers a peaceful retreat where you can relax on soft sand and soak in the beauty of the turquoise waters. The calm and clear waters make it an ideal spot for swimming and snorkeling, allowing you to discover the vibrant marine life inhabiting nearby coral reefs.

Devonshire Parish also offers a range of recreational activities. Golf enthusiasts can tee off at the Belmont Hills Golf Club, a picturesque course that winds its way through rolling hills and offers stunning views of the island. Tennis courts, cricket fields, and sports clubs are also available for those looking to stay active during their visit.

Culinary delights await in Devonshire Parish, with various restaurants and cafes offering a taste of Bermuda's diverse cuisine. From local seafood delicacies to international flavors, something suits every palate. Enjoy fresh fish dishes, indulge in a traditional afternoon tea, or savor the flavors of Bermuda's famous fish chowder.

Devonshire Parish's central location makes it a convenient base for exploring other parts of the island. Its proximity to the capital city of Hamilton allows easy access to shopping districts, cultural attractions, and vibrant nightlife.

With its blend of natural beauty, historical charm, and recreational opportunities, Devonshire Parish offers a well-rounded experience for visitors. Whether you're strolling through the botanical gardens, delving into history at Verdmont House, or simply enjoying the tranquility of Devonshire Bay, this Parish promises a memorable and enriching experience in the heart of Bermuda.

Pembroke Parish

Pembroke Parish, located on the main island of Bermuda, is a vibrant and dynamic region that serves as the gateway to the island's capital, Hamilton. Known for its mix of residential, commercial, and cultural attractions, Pembroke Parish offers a captivating blend of history, entertainment, and natural beauty.

At the heart of Pembroke Parish lies Hamilton, the bustling capital city of Bermuda. Here, visitors can immerse themselves in the city's vibrant energy and explore its vibrant streets lined with shops, restaurants, and cultural landmarks. Front Street, the city's main thoroughfare, offers a plethora of shopping opportunities, from high-end boutiques to local artisanal craft stores. Experience the city's lively atmosphere as you dine at waterfront restaurants, enjoy street performances, or simply take in the stunning views of Hamilton Harbour.

For history enthusiasts, the Bermuda Historical Society Museum is a must-visit attraction in Pembroke Parish. Housed in a charming Georgian-style building, this museum showcases artifacts and exhibits that tell the story of Bermuda's rich heritage. Discover the island's maritime history, explore Bermuda's cultural traditions, and gain insights into the lives of its early inhabitants.

Nature lovers will appreciate the stunning landscapes found within Pembroke Parish. Victoria Park, a serene oasis in the heart of Hamilton, offers lush gardens, shaded pathways, and a tranquil pond. Take a leisurely stroll, have a picnic, or simply enjoy the peaceful surroundings. Nearby, the Bermuda National

Gallery showcases a diverse collection of local and international art, providing a cultural escape for art enthusiasts.

Pembroke Parish is also home to Admiralty House Park, a hidden gem nestled along the coastline. This picturesque park features scenic walking trails, secluded coves, and the historic Admiralty House itself. Take a refreshing swim in the turquoise waters, explore the remnants of a once-secret naval facility, or simply relax on the rocky shoreline while soaking up the breathtaking views.

Culinary adventures abound in Pembroke Parish, with an array of restaurants and cafes offering a range of flavors to suit every palate. Sample local delicacies, such as Bermuda fish chowder or the famous fish sandwich, or indulge in international cuisine at one of the many gourmet eateries scattered throughout the Parish.

Pembroke Parish's central location makes it an ideal base for exploring other parts of Bermuda. Convenient transportation links allow easy access to the island's beautiful beaches, historical sites, and natural wonders.

With its vibrant city life, cultural attractions, and natural beauty, Pembroke Parish offers a dynamic experience for visitors. Whether you're strolling along the streets of Hamilton, exploring historical landmarks, or enjoying the tranquility of its parks and coastlines, Pembroke Parish promises a memorable and multifaceted journey through the heart of Bermuda.

Paget Parish

Paget Parish, located in the central part of Bermuda, is a beautiful region known for its stunning beaches, picturesque landscapes, and historical landmarks. Named after William Paget, the 4th Baron Paget of Beaudesert, this Parish offers a tranquil escape and a wealth of attractions for visitors to explore.

One of the highlights of Paget Parish is Elbow Beach, a breathtaking stretch of pink sand beach that is considered one of the most beautiful on the island. With its crystal-clear turquoise waters and gentle surf, Elbow Beach is perfect for swimming, sunbathing, and beachcombing. The surrounding area also boasts luxury resorts and hotels, offering visitors a chance to relax in style while enjoying the stunning ocean views.

For a taste of Bermuda's natural beauty, head to the Botanical Gardens in Paget Parish. These expansive gardens feature a wide variety of plant species, including colorful tropical flowers, lush palm trees, and aromatic herbs. Take a leisurely stroll through the well-manicured pathways, visit the sensory garden, and admire the tranquil ponds and water features. The gardens also house the Camden House, an elegant colonial mansion that serves as the official residence of Bermuda's Premier.

History enthusiasts will appreciate the wealth of historical sites in Paget Parish. The Bermuda Underwater Exploration Institute (BUEI) offers a fascinating journey into Bermuda's maritime heritage through interactive exhibits and displays. Explore the history of shipwrecks, learn about underwater exploration, and discover the diverse marine life that inhabits Bermuda's waters.

Another significant historical site in Paget Parish is the Perot Post Office and Historical Museum. Housed in a charming 17th-century building, this museum showcases the island's postal history and exhibits artifacts that shed light on Bermuda's past. Explore the collection of stamps, postal equipment, and historic documents that tell the story of the island's communication evolution.

Golf enthusiasts will find paradise in Paget Parish at the Belmont Hills Golf Club. This scenic golf course offers stunning views of the ocean and the surrounding landscapes as you tee off amidst lush green fairways and rolling hills. Enjoy a challenging round of golf while taking in the beauty of Bermuda's natural surroundings.

Culinary delights await in Paget Parish, with a range of restaurants and eateries offering a variety of cuisine to satisfy every palate. Indulge in fresh seafood dishes, savor local specialties like fish chowder and rockfish, or sample international flavors at gourmet establishments.

Paget Parish's central location makes it an ideal base for exploring other parts of Bermuda. Its proximity to the capital city of Hamilton allows for easy access to shopping districts, cultural attractions, and vibrant nightlife.

With its stunning beaches, botanical gardens, historical landmarks, and recreational opportunities, Paget Parish promises an unforgettable experience in the heart of Bermuda. Whether you're lounging on Elbow Beach, exploring the exhibits at BUEI, or immersing yourself in the island's natural beauty at the Botanical Gardens, Paget Parish invites visitors to embrace the tranquility and charm of the island.

Warwick Parish

Warwick Parish, situated on the western part of Bermuda's main island, is a beautiful region known for its stunning beaches, picturesque landscapes, and historical landmarks. With its natural beauty and cultural attractions blend, Warwick Parish offers visitors a chance to relax, explore, and immerse themselves in Bermuda's charm.

One of the main highlights of Warwick Parish is Warwick Long Bay, a pristine stretch of pink sand beach that is considered one of the island's most beautiful. With its turquoise waters and dramatic rocky outcrops, this beach offers a picturesque setting for swimming, sunbathing, and leisurely walks along the shore. The beach is bordered by dunes and lush vegetation, providing a serene and secluded atmosphere.

Nature enthusiasts will appreciate the diverse landscapes found within Warwick Parish. South Shore Park offers stunning Atlantic Ocean vistas and a network of scenic trails that wind through picturesque coastal landscapes, limestone formations, and hidden coves. Explore the park on foot or rent a bicycle to discover its hidden gems and breathtaking views.

Warwick Pond, a protected nature reserve in the Parish, is a haven for birdwatchers and nature lovers. This serene wetland provides a home for various bird species, including herons, egrets, and ducks. Stroll along the trails surrounding the pond, and keep an eye out for other wildlife that calls this peaceful oasis their home.

For history buffs, the historic Astwood Cove offers a glimpse into Bermuda's past. This secluded cove was once a hub for the island's early settlers, and remnants of their homes and structures can still be found scattered around the area. Explore the ruins and imagine the lives of the early settlers who once called this place home.

Warwick Parish also offers a range of culinary delights. Restaurants and eateries in the area serve a variety of cuisine, from fresh seafood to international flavors. Sample traditional Bermudian dishes such as fish cakes, fish chowder, and Bermuda fish sandwiches, or indulge in gourmet dining experiences at one of the many establishments in the Parish.

Warwick Parish's central location makes it an ideal base for exploring other parts of Bermuda. Its proximity to the popular tourist destinations of Southampton and Paget Parishes allows for easy access to additional beaches, golf courses, and cultural attractions.

With its stunning beaches, natural reserves, historical sites, and culinary offerings, Warwick Parish promises a memorable experience for visitors. Whether you're enjoying the beauty of Warwick Long Bay, discovering the hidden gems of South Shore Park, or indulging in the flavors of Bermudian cuisine, Warwick Parish invites you to unwind and embrace the enchanting landscapes of Bermuda.

Southampton Parish

Southampton Parish, located on the western end of Bermuda's main island, is a picturesque region known for its stunning beaches, scenic landscapes, and historical landmarks. With its combination of natural beauty and cultural attractions, Southampton Parish offers visitors a captivating experience and a chance to immerse themselves in the island's charm.

One of the highlights of Southampton Parish is Horseshoe Bay Beach, an iconic stretch of pink sand that consistently ranks among the world's most beautiful beaches. With its crystal-clear turquoise waters and dramatic rock formations, Horseshoe Bay Beach provides an idyllic setting for sunbathing, swimming, and snorkeling. The beach's horseshoe-shaped curve offers calm and gentle waves, making it perfect for families and water enthusiasts of all ages.

For a taste of Bermuda's history, visit Gibbs Hill Lighthouse, which stands tall as one of the oldest cast-iron lighthouses in the world. Climb the 185 steps to the top of the lighthouse for panoramic views of the island and the sparkling Atlantic Ocean. Enjoy breathtaking vistas of Southampton Parish and beyond, as the lighthouse offers a unique vantage point to appreciate Bermuda's natural beauty.

Nature lovers will find solace in Southampton Parish's many parks and reserves. The Southampton Parish Park, located on the outskirts of the Parish, is a serene oasis that offers lush green spaces, walking trails, and picnic areas. Enjoy a leisurely stroll through the park, surrounded by native flora and fauna, or find a quiet spot to relax and enjoy the peaceful ambiance.

For golf enthusiasts, Southampton Parish is home to the prestigious Port Royal Golf Course. This championship golf course, known for its challenging layout and stunning ocean views, has hosted several international tournaments, including the PGA Grand Slam of Golf. Tee off amidst lush fairways, rugged cliffs, and panoramic vistas, and experience golfing at its finest in this picturesque setting.

Culinary delights await in Southampton Parish, with various restaurants and eateries offering a range of flavors. Sample fresh seafood dishes, indulge in international cuisine, or savor traditional Bermudian specialties such as fish chowder or fish sandwiches. Many establishments in the Parish offer oceanfront dining, allowing visitors to enjoy their meals while taking in the breathtaking coastal views.

Southampton Parish's central location makes it an ideal base for exploring other parts of Bermuda. Its proximity to the Royal Naval Dockyard, Hamilton, and other popular destinations allows for easy access to additional attractions, shopping districts, and cultural experiences.

Southampton Parish promises an unforgettable experience for visitors. Whether you're basking in the beauty of Horseshoe Bay Beach, admiring the views from Gibbs Hill Lighthouse, or indulging in the flavors of Bermudian cuisine, Southampton Parish invites you to embrace the serenity and splendor of Bermuda's western coast.

Sandys Parish

Sandys Parish, located on the westernmost tip of Bermuda's main island, is a captivating region known for its natural beauty, historical sites, and charming coastal communities. With its pristine beaches, lush parks, and cultural landmarks, Sandys Parish offers visitors a unique and enriching experience.

One of the main attractions of Sandys Parish is the stunning coastline, which features some of Bermuda's most picturesque beaches. The most famous of these is the renowned Horseshoe Bay Beach, with its powdery pink sand and crystal-clear turquoise waters. This idyllic beach is a haven for sunbathers, swimmers, and snorkelers, offering a tranquil setting to relax and soak up the sun. The adjacent Warwick Long Bay Beach and Chaplin Bay Beach also offer beautiful stretches of sand and inviting waters for visitors to enjoy.

Another notable landmark in Sandys Parish is the Royal Naval Dockyard. This historical complex was once the principal base of the British Navy in the Western Atlantic. Today, it has been transformed into a vibrant cultural and entertainment hub. Explore the maritime museum, visit the craft markets, or take a leisurely stroll along the waterfront promenade. The Dockyard is also home to the National Museum of Bermuda, which showcases the island's rich history and heritage.

Nature enthusiasts will appreciate the scenic parks and reserves in Sandys Parish. The Somerset Long Bay Park offers a peaceful retreat with its sandy beaches, shaded picnic areas, and nature trails. Enjoy a leisurely walk along the coastline, go for a refreshing swim, or simply relax in the tranquility of the surroundings. For a taste of Bermuda's flora and fauna, visit the Heydon Trust Park, which features well-manicured gardens and a diverse collection of plant species.

History comes alive in Sandys Parish at the historic Gibbs Hill Lighthouse. Built-in 1846, this cast-iron lighthouse stands tall on a hilltop, offering panoramic views of the island and the surrounding waters. Climb to the top of the lighthouse for breathtaking vistas and gain insights into Bermuda's maritime history.

Culinary experiences in Sandys Parish are equally delightful. Local restaurants and eateries offer a range of dining options, from fresh seafood dishes to international cuisine. Sample traditional Bermudian favorites such as fish chowder or fish sandwiches, or savor the flavors of gourmet dining in charming seaside settings.

Sandys Parish's central location makes it an ideal base for exploring other parts of Bermuda. Its proximity to Hamilton and other popular destinations allows for convenient access to additional attractions, shopping districts, and cultural experiences.

Sandys Parish promises a memorable experience for visitors. Whether you're basking in the sun at Horseshoe Bay Beach, immersing yourself in Bermuda's maritime history at the Royal Naval Dockyard, or exploring the parks and gardens, Sandys Parish invites you to discover the captivating allure of Bermuda's western coast.

Other Islands in Bermuda

While Bermuda's main island is a captivating destination in itself, the archipelago is also home to several smaller islands that offer unique experiences and natural wonders. These smaller islands, scattered throughout the Atlantic Ocean, allow visitors to explore secluded beaches, encounter diverse wildlife, and immerse themselves in Bermuda's rich marine environment. Here are some of the other islands in Bermuda that are worth exploring:

St. George's Island: Located in St. George's Parish, St. George's Island is a UNESCO World Heritage Site and the historical heart of Bermuda. This charming island is home to the town of St. George, the oldest continuously inhabited English town in the New World. Visitors can wander through its narrow, winding streets, visit historic sites such as St. Peter's Church and the Unfinished Church, and explore the centuries-old forts that once protected the island from invaders.

Nonsuch Island: Situated in St. George's Parish, Nonsuch Island is a nature reserve and sanctuary for endangered species. The island is named after the ship that brought the first settlers to Bermuda in 1609. Access to the island is restricted, but visitors can take guided tours to learn about its conservation efforts and view rare bird species, including the Bermuda petrel, also known as the cahow.

Cooper's Island: Located in St. George's Parish, Cooper's Island is a hidden gem with secluded beaches, nature trails, and stunning vistas. The island is home to a nature reserve and a protected area for wildlife, making it a haven for birdwatchers and nature lovers. Explore the walking trails, relax on the pristine beaches, or go snorkeling to discover the vibrant marine life and coral reefs that surround the island.

Somerset Island: Situated in Sandys Parish, Somerset Island is known for its picturesque landscapes and tranquil beaches. The island is connected to the main island by Somerset Bridge, the smallest drawbridge in the world. Visitors can enjoy leisurely walks along the coastline, take in the panoramic views from the nearby parks, or explore the charming village of Somerset.

Ireland Island: Located in Sandys Parish, Ireland Island is a predominantly residential area that is home to the Royal Naval Dockyard. The Dockyard, a former British Navy base, has been transformed into a lively cultural and entertainment hub. Explore its historical sites, museums, craft markets, and waterfront restaurants. Ireland Island is also known for its picturesque surroundings and stunning sunsets.

Paget Island: Situated in Paget Parish, Paget Island is a small, uninhabited island that offers stunning views of the Great Sound and the surrounding waters. Accessible by boat, visitors can enjoy picnicking, snorkeling, and swimming in its secluded coves and clear waters. The island is also home to the Martello Tower, a 19th-century fortification offering panoramic coastline views.

Castle Island: Located near the western tip of Bermuda's main island, Castle Island is a small islet known for its iconic Fort Scaur. The fort offers panoramic views of the Great Sound and provides insight into Bermuda's military history. Visitors can explore the fort's exhibits, stroll along the ramparts, and enjoy the scenic surroundings.

These smaller islands in Bermuda offer a diverse range of experiences, from historical exploration to nature immersion. Whether you're discovering the UNESCO World Heritage site of St. George's Island, observing rare bird species on Nonsuch Island, or basking in the tranquility of Somerset Island's beaches, each of these islands provides a unique and unforgettable adventure. Embark on a journey to Bermuda's other islands and uncover the hidden gems and natural wonders that await.

Ruby Shawn

TOP ATTRACTIONS IN

BERMUDA

Bermuda, with its breathtaking landscapes, rich history, and vibrant culture, is a destination that offers a plethora of attractions for visitors to explore. From stunning pink sand beaches to historical landmarks, the island presents an array of experiences that cater to every traveler's interests. Whether you're seeking outdoor adventures, cultural immersion, or simply relaxation, Bermuda has something to captivate you.

Explore the iconic Horseshoe Bay Beach with its crystal-clear waters, visit the UNESCO World Heritage Site of St. George's, or delve into the fascinating history at the Royal Naval Dockyard. Discover the natural wonders of the Crystal Caves, go snorkeling in the vibrant coral reefs, or wander through the charming streets of Hamilton, the capital city. With its natural beauty and cultural heritage blend, Bermuda's top attractions promise an unforgettable journey into this enchanting island paradise.

Horseshoe Bay Beach

Horseshoe Bay Beach, located on the southern coast of Bermuda's main island, is a world-renowned destination known for its stunning beauty and pristine pink sand. With its crystal-clear turquoise waters, dramatic rock formations, and crescent-shaped shoreline, Horseshoe Bay Beach is a paradise for beach lovers and nature enthusiasts.

The beach gets its name from its unique horseshoe shape, which provides a natural barrier and creates calm, gentle waves, making it an ideal spot for swimming and relaxation. The soft, pink sand adds to the beach's allure, creating a striking contrast against the vibrant blue hues of the ocean.

Horseshoe Bay Beach offers something for everyone. Sunbathers can lounge on the warm sand, basking in the island's abundant sunshine. The beach's wide expanse ensures plenty of space for everyone to find a cozy spot to unwind and soak up the tranquil atmosphere.

For those seeking adventure, Horseshoe Bay Beach offers opportunities for snorkeling and exploring marine life. The clear waters provide excellent visibility, allowing visitors to discover the vibrant coral reefs and colorful fish that inhabit the area. Snorkeling gear can be rented on-site, making it convenient for visitors to dive into the underwater wonders of the beach.

The beach is also equipped with facilities to ensure a comfortable experience for visitors. Changing rooms, bathrooms, and showers are available, making it convenient for beachgoers to freshen up after a day of sun and sand. Beach chairs and umbrellas can be rented for added convenience and shade.

Horseshoe Bay Beach is not just a place to relax and swim; it also offers opportunities for exploration and adventure. Adjacent to the beach, there are rugged coastal trails that lead to hidden coves and stunning vistas. Walking along these trails allows visitors to appreciate the raw beauty of Bermuda's coastline and capture breathtaking views of the Atlantic Ocean.

The beach's popularity can lead to crowds during peak seasons. Still, it remains spacious enough to find a peaceful corner to enjoy the surroundings. Additionally, the beach's size and amenities make it suitable for families, providing a safe and enjoyable environment for children to play and build sandcastles.

Whether you're seeking a tranquil escape, thrilling water activities, or simply want to marvel at the natural beauty of Bermuda, Horseshoe Bay Beach offers an unforgettable experience. From the soft pink sand to the turquoise waters, this iconic beach beckons visitors to unwind, explore, and create lasting memories in one of the most stunning coastal settings in the world.

Royal Naval Dockyard

The Royal Naval Dockyard, located on Ireland Island in Sandys Parish, is a historic landmark and a vibrant cultural hub in Bermuda. Once a strategic naval base for the British Navy in the Western Atlantic, the Dockyard has been transformed into a bustling destination that offers a wealth of attractions, entertainment, and shopping experiences.

The history of the Royal Naval Dockyard dates back to the early 19th century when it served as a crucial outpost for the British Navy. Today, visitors can explore the Dockyard's rich maritime heritage through various exhibits and museums. The National Museum of Bermuda, housed within the Dockyard's walls, showcases artifacts, interactive displays, and galleries that chronicle the island's history, from its early settlement to its naval past.

One of the major draws of the Royal Naval Dockyard is its lively waterfront area. Visitors can stroll along the picturesque harbor, where colorful buildings and historic architecture create a charming atmosphere. The Dockyard boasts an array of restaurants, cafes, and bars, offering a diverse range of culinary delights, from fresh seafood to international cuisine. Outdoor seating allows guests to enjoy their meals while taking panoramic waterfront views.

Shopping enthusiasts will find plenty to indulge in at the Dockyard's numerous retail outlets and craft markets. From high-end boutiques to local artisans selling handmade goods, the Dockyard offers a range of shopping experiences. Browse for unique Bermuda-inspired souvenirs, jewelry, artwork, and clothing, or visit the craft market to support local craftsmen and artisans.

The Dockyard also hosts various cultural events and festivals annually, showcasing Bermuda's vibrant arts and entertainment scene. From live music performances to art exhibitions and cultural celebrations, something always happens at the Dockyard that showcases the island's talent and creativity.

For those seeking family-friendly activities, the Dockyard offers attractions such as the Bermuda Fun Golf, a mini-golf course with a stunning ocean backdrop, and the Dolphin Quest, where visitors can swim and interact with dolphins in a controlled environment. There are also opportunities for water sports, including jet skiing, parasailing, and kayaking, providing adrenaline-pumping adventures for thrill-seekers.

The Royal Naval Dockyard is easily accessible from other parts of Bermuda via ferry, bus, or taxi, making it a convenient destination for day trips or longer stays. Its location on the island's western end offers breathtaking views of the Great Sound and the surrounding waters.

Whether you're interested in history, shopping, dining, or simply soaking up the vibrant atmosphere, the Royal Naval Dockyard in Bermuda offers a captivating blend of past and present. Explore its museums, wander along the waterfront, indulge in local cuisine, or immerse yourself in the island's arts and culture. The Dockyard is a must-visit destination showcasing Bermuda's unique charm and heritage.

St. Peter's Church

Located in the historic town of St. George's, St. Peter's Church is a stunning example of Bermudian architecture and an iconic landmark that showcases the island's rich religious heritage. Founded in 1612, the church is the oldest Anglican church in the Western Hemisphere. Its pristine white walls and elegant bell tower are a sight to behold.

St. Peter's Church has a fascinating history that is closely intertwined with that of Bermuda itself. The church was originally built as a wooden structure in 1612 and was rebuilt twice over the following centuries due to damage from storms and fires. The current building dates back to the early 18th century, and its striking design and interior are a testament to the skill of Bermudian craftsmen and artisans.

Visitors to St. Peter's Church can explore the church's rich history and stunning architecture through various exhibits and displays. The church's interior features elegant wooden pews, gleaming brass fixtures, and intricate stained-glass windows that depict biblical scenes and local motifs. The church's graveyard, located outside, is also a fascinating place to explore, with gravestones dating back to the early days of Bermuda's settlement.

One of the most striking features of St. Peter's Church is its stunning bell tower, which rises above the surrounding landscape and provides stunning views of St. George's and the surrounding waters. The tower houses a collection of historic bells, some dating back to the 1600s, and is still rung for special occasions and events.

St. Peter's Church is also an active place of worship, and visitors can attend services and events throughout the year. The church's choir, composed of local singers, performs regularly, adding to the church's tranquil and peaceful atmosphere.

The church is easily accessible from other parts of Bermuda and is a popular destination for tourists and locals alike. Visitors can explore the church on their own or take a guided tour with one of knowledgeable volunteers who offer insights into the church's history and significance.

For those interested in history, architecture, and religious heritage, St. Peter's Church in Bermuda is a must-visit destination. Its stunning design, rich history, and tranquil atmosphere make it an unforgettable experience for all who visit.

Bermuda Aquarium, Museum & Zoo

Nestled in picturesque Flatts Village, the Bermuda Aquarium, Museum & Zoo (BAMZ) is a captivating destination that offers visitors a unique opportunity to explore the island's diverse marine life, learn about its natural history, and encounter a range of fascinating animals from around the world.

The aquarium is home to a stunning array of marine species, showcasing the vibrant and colorful underwater world that surrounds Bermuda. Visitors can wander through the exhibits and marvel at the beauty of tropical fish, mesmerizing coral reefs, and intriguing marine creatures. From graceful sea turtles to playful seals, the aquarium provides an up-close encounter with marine life, allowing visitors to learn about their habitats, behaviors, and conservation efforts.

Beyond the aquarium, the museum offers a deeper exploration of Bermuda's natural history and cultural heritage. Exhibits showcase the island's geological formation, the diversity of its flora and fauna, and the impact of human activities on the environment. Visitors can better understand Bermuda's unique ecosystem and the importance of preserving its delicate balance.

One of the highlights of the Bermuda Aquarium, Museum & Zoo is its zoo, where various animals worldwide reside. From majestic lions to colorful birds and playful lemurs, the zoo provides an opportunity to observe and learn about multiple species in a carefully designed and naturalistic environment. Educational presentations and feeding sessions further enhance the experience, allowing visitors to gain insights into the animals' behaviors and conservation efforts.

The BAMZ is not just a place for observation; it also plays a vital role in conservation and research. The facility is involved in numerous initiatives to protect and preserve Bermuda's natural resources and raise awareness about environmental issues. Visitors can learn about these efforts and how they can contribute to conserving the island's unique ecosystems.

The BAMZ offers educational programs for visitors of all ages, including guided tours, interactive exhibits, and hands-on activities. Families and school groups can participate in workshops, nature walks, and educational presentations that provide a deeper understanding of Bermuda's natural wonders.

Conveniently located and easily accessible, the Bermuda Aquarium, Museum & Zoo offers a captivating and enriching experience for nature enthusiasts, families, and anyone interested in exploring the wonders of Bermuda's marine and terrestrial ecosystems. Whether it's marveling at the colorful fish, learning about conservation efforts, or observing animals from around the world, a visit to the BAMZ is a journey into the beauty and diversity of the natural world.

Crystal Caves

Located in the parish of Hamilton, Bermuda's Crystal Caves are a natural wonder that never fails to impress visitors. Two local boys discovered the caves in 1907, and they have since become one of Bermuda's most popular tourist attractions.

Visitors to Crystal Caves are transported into an underground world of natural beauty and wonder. Descending down a staircase, visitors find themselves in a chamber adorned with stalactites and stalagmites formed over millions of years by the slow drip of water. The crystal-clear water in the caves is so pristine that you can see the bottom, revealing a floor filled with more stalactites and stalagmites.

The highlight of the visit is the breathtaking Crystal Lake, which shimmers with a mesmerizing, almost otherworldly turquoise color. The lake is deep and mysterious, and visitors can observe its crystal-clear waters from a pontoon bridge that extends across its center. As sunlight filters through the cracks and crevices in the cave's ceiling, it creates a stunning array of reflections on the water, casting shimmering patterns across the cave's walls.

The guided tour of Crystal Caves provides an insight into the geology and history of the caves, including the legends and stories that have been passed down through generations of Bermudians. Visitors can also learn about the scientific research being conducted in the caves, which is helping to shed light on the island's geological history.

Crystal Caves is a destination that appeals to all ages, offering a glimpse into the natural wonders of Bermuda and a chance to appreciate the island's unique geology. The caves are also accessible to visitors with mobility challenges, with handrails and a smooth walkway leading through the caves.

A visit to Crystal Caves is an unforgettable experience that leaves visitors with a newfound appreciation for the beauty and complexity of the natural world. The caves are a testament to the power of nature and the wonder of discovery, providing a window into a world that has been hidden beneath the surface of Bermuda for millions of years.

Gibbs Hill Lighthouse

Perched atop a hill in Southampton Parish, Bermuda, Gibbs Hill Lighthouse stands tall as a symbol of both maritime heritage and panoramic beauty. Built-in 1844, this iconic cast-iron structure has become a beloved landmark and a must-visit destination for tourists and locals alike.

Ascending the winding staircase to the top of Gibbs Hill Lighthouse is a journey through time and history. The lighthouse was constructed to guide ships navigating Bermuda's treacherous reefs, providing a crucial beacon of light to ensure safe passage. Today, it serves as a fascinating testament to Bermuda's maritime past and offers visitors an opportunity to learn about the island's maritime heritage.

Reaching the top of the lighthouse rewards visitors with awe-inspiring views of Bermuda's picturesque landscapes. Panoramic vistas stretch out in every direction, encompassing turquoise waters, verdant hills, and an enchanting coastline. On a clear day, you can even spot neighboring islands dotting the horizon. The breathtaking scenery makes Gibbs Hill Lighthouse a perfect spot for capturing memorable photographs or simply taking in the island's natural beauty.

To enhance the experience, Gibbs Hill Lighthouse features a small museum inside its base. Exhibits showcase artifacts and photographs that provide insights into the lighthouse's history and its importance in Bermuda's maritime navigation. Visitors can learn about the technology and methods used to operate the lighthouse in its early days and better understand its vital role in ensuring the safety of ships traversing Bermuda's waters.

After exploring the lighthouse and museum, visitors can relax and indulge in a meal or refreshments at the nearby Gibbs Hill Lighthouse Restaurant. With its charming ambiance and stunning views, the restaurant offers a delightful culinary experience accompanied by the gentle sea breeze and sweeping vistas.

Gibbs Hill Lighthouse is easily accessible by public transportation or taxi, and its location makes it a popular stop for tourists exploring the western part of the island. Whether you're a history enthusiast, a nature lover, or simply seeking breathtaking views, visiting Gibbs Hill Lighthouse is an enriching experience that allows you to connect with Bermuda's seafaring past while marveling at its natural splendor.

Standing tall as a symbol of both navigational prowess and scenic beauty, Gibbs Hill Lighthouse invites visitors to explore its history, ascend to its pinnacle, and embrace the sweeping panoramas that unfold before their eyes. It's a destination that showcases the timeless allure of Bermuda and offers a glimpse into the island's captivating maritime heritage.

Bermuda Underwater Exploration Institute

Nestled on the shores of Hamilton Harbour in Bermuda, the Bermuda Underwater Exploration Institute (BUEI) is a fascinating destination that offers visitors a unique opportunity to dive into the wonders of the underwater world. With its interactive exhibits, educational programs, and captivating displays, the BUEI is a hub for ocean exploration and conservation.

The BUEI takes visitors on a captivating journey through Bermuda's marine ecosystem and the mysteries of the deep sea. The institute's exhibits showcase a diverse range of marine life, from colorful coral reefs to mesmerizing fish species. Visitors can learn about the delicate balance of marine ecosystems, the importance of conservation, and the impact of human activities on the ocean.

One of the highlights of the BUEI is its state-of-the-art Ocean Discovery Centre, where visitors can immerse themselves in a virtual underwater experience. Through interactive displays and cutting-edge technology, visitors can explore the ocean's depths, encounter marine creatures, and gain a deeper understanding of the complexities of marine life.

The BUEI also hosts a variety of educational programs and events for visitors of all ages. From lectures and workshops to film screenings and guided tours, there are numerous opportunities to learn about marine science, marine archaeology, and the importance of ocean conservation. The institute's knowledgeable staff and scientists are on hand to answer questions and provide valuable insights into the underwater world.

For those seeking hands-on experiences, the BUEI offers dive programs and snorkeling excursions, allowing visitors to explore Bermuda's vibrant reefs and encounter marine life up close. Guided tours of the island's shipwrecks are also available, providing a glimpse into Bermuda's maritime history and the fascinating world that lies beneath its waters.

The BUEI is a place of discovery and education and a hub for research and conservation efforts. The institute collaborates with local and international organizations to study and protect Bermuda's marine environment. Visitors can learn about ongoing research projects and the steps being taken to safeguard the ocean for future generations.

Conveniently located and easily accessible, the Bermuda Underwater Exploration Institute offers a captivating and immersive experience for ocean enthusiasts, families, and anyone curious about the wonders of the deep. Whether you're exploring interactive exhibits, attending educational programs, or embarking on underwater adventures, a visit to the BUEI is a journey into the fascinating world of the ocean, revealing its beauty, fragility, and the need to protect it for generations to come.

Spittal Pond Nature Reserve

Nestled on the southeastern coast of Bermuda, Spittal Pond Nature Reserve is a serene and enchanting destination that captivates visitors with its untouched beauty and abundant wildlife. As the largest nature reserve on the island, it offers a peaceful escape from the hustle and bustle of city life, inviting visitors to immerse themselves in the tranquility of nature.

Spanning over 60 acres, Spittal Pond Nature Reserve encompasses a variety of habitats, including pristine coastlines, wetlands, woodlands, and open grassy areas. The reserve's diverse ecosystem provides a haven for many plant and animal species, making it a paradise for nature lovers and birdwatchers.

One of the main attractions of Spittal Pond Nature Reserve is its picturesque walking trails that wind their way through the reserve, offering breathtaking views of the coastline, lush vegetation, and peaceful ponds. As visitors explore the trails, they may encounter native birds, including herons, egrets, cormorants, and migratory species that make a stopover in Bermuda during their journeys.

Spittal Pond Nature Reserve is also home to several historical landmarks, adding to its allure. At the eastern end of the reserve, visitors can find the remains of a 17th-century gunpowder magazine, a reminder of Bermuda's military past. The nearby Spittal Pond is a serene saltwater pond surrounded by mangroves. Visitors can observe the unique ecosystem that thrives in this coastal wetland.

Visiting Spittal Pond Nature Reserve provides an opportunity to reconnect with nature and enjoy the simple pleasures of walking, birdwatching, and picnicking amidst beautiful surroundings. The reserve offers a sense of tranquility and solitude, allowing visitors to unwind and rejuvenate their spirits.

It is important to note that Spittal Pond Nature Reserve is a protected area, and visitors are encouraged to respect its delicate ecosystem. By staying on designated trails and avoiding disturbance to wildlife and vegetation, visitors can contribute to preserving this natural treasure.

Spittal Pond Nature Reserve is easily accessible by public transportation or car, and parking facilities are available. Whether you're a nature enthusiast, a bird lover, or simply seeking a peaceful retreat, a visit to Spittal Pond Nature Reserve is an opportunity to immerse yourself in Bermuda's natural beauty and discover the wonders of its untouched landscapes.

Botanical Gardens

Nestled in the heart of Paget Parish, Bermuda's Botanical Gardens is a breathtaking oasis that showcases the island's vibrant flora and offers visitors a serene retreat from the hustle and bustle of everyday life. Spanning 36 acres, these meticulously manicured gardens are a paradise for nature lovers and a feast for the senses.

The Botanical Gardens boast a diverse collection of plant species from Bermuda and worldwide. As visitors wander through the gardens, they are greeted by a kaleidoscope of colors, fragrances, and textures. The gardens provide a rich tapestry of botanical wonders, from exotic orchids and tropical palms to delicate roses and aromatic herbs.

One of the highlights of the Botanical Gardens is the Sensory Garden, designed to engage all five senses. Here, visitors can touch the velvety petals of flowers, inhale the intoxicating scents of blooming plants, listen to the gentle rustle of leaves, and even taste some of the edible herbs and fruits grown in the garden. The Sensory Garden offers a unique and immersive experience, allowing visitors to connect with nature in a deeply sensory way.

The Botanical Gardens also feature a stunning greenhouse, home to various exotic plants from different regions of the world. Step inside, and you'll find yourself transported to lush rainforests or arid desert landscapes, depending on the section of the greenhouse you explore. It's a chance to witness the incredible diversity of plant life that exists beyond Bermuda's shores.

In addition to its floral displays, the Botanical Gardens is also a place of cultural and historical significance. The Camden House, a beautifully restored mansion within the gardens, serves as the Visitor Centre and offers insights into Bermuda's architectural heritage. Exhibits showcase the island's history, culture, and the gardens' important role in preserving its natural beauty.

Visitors to the Botanical Gardens can take leisurely strolls along the winding pathways, relax on benches surrounded by blooming flowers, or enjoy a picnic in the shade of majestic trees. The gardens also host events and concerts throughout the year, providing a delightful backdrop for cultural and social gatherings.

Conveniently located and easily accessible, the Botanical Gardens offers a serene and enchanting escape into the world of plants and flowers. Whether you're a botany enthusiast, a nature lover, or simply seeking a tranquil spot to unwind, visiting the Botanical Gardens is an opportunity to immerse yourself in Bermuda's natural splendor and witness the captivating beauty of its flora.

Historical Sites and Museums

Bermuda, an enchanting island in the Atlantic Ocean, is steeped in a rich history that dates back centuries. Exploring its historical sites and museums is like embarking on a captivating journey through time, where visitors can discover the stories, artifacts, and cultural treasures that have shaped the island's identity.

The Town of St. George, a UNESCO World Heritage site, is a must-visit destination for history enthusiasts. Established in 1612, it is the oldest continually inhabited English town in the New World. The town's winding streets are lined with charming colonial buildings that reflect its rich architectural heritage. At the heart of St. George is King's Square, where visitors can explore notable landmarks like the State House, the oldest stone building in Bermuda. The State House, once a meeting place for Bermuda's parliament, now serves as a museum that offers a glimpse into the island's political history.

St. Peter's Church, located in St. George, is another historical gem. Dating back to 1612, it is one of the oldest continuously used Anglican churches in the Western Hemisphere. The church's architectural splendor and tranquil atmosphere transport visitors to a bygone era. At the same time, its burial grounds hold the final resting place of notable figures from Bermuda's past.

The Royal Naval Dockyard, a former British naval base, is a hub of historical significance and cultural exploration. This sprawling complex has been transformed into a vibrant center featuring museums, art galleries, craft markets, and restaurants. The National Museum of Bermuda, housed within the Dockyard, provides a comprehensive overview of the island's history.

Exhibits showcase Bermuda's maritime heritage, including shipwreck discoveries, artifacts, and interactive displays that delve into the island's role in the Atlantic slave trade. Visitors can also explore the historic fortifications within the Dockyard, such as the imposing Keep of the Royal Naval Dockyard and the iconic Clocktower Mall.

Bermuda's maritime history comes to life at the Bermuda Maritime Museum, located within the grounds of the Royal Naval Dockyard. Housed in a restored fortress, the museum offers a captivating journey through Bermuda's seafaring past. It showcases a wealth of maritime artifacts, shipwreck discoveries, and exhibits highlighting the island's connection to the sea. From model ships to interactive displays, visitors can delve into the challenges faced by sailors navigating Bermuda's treacherous reefs and explore the island's role in maritime commerce and exploration.

For those interested in military history, Bermuda's forts offer a fascinating glimpse into the island's defensive strategies. Fort Hamilton, Fort Scaur, and Fort St. Catherine are among the notable forts that dot Bermuda's coastline. With their commanding views and architectural splendor, these structures stand as a testament to the island's military past. Visitors can explore their ramparts, tunnels, and artillery placements while immersing themselves in Bermuda's history.

Bermuda's cultural heritage is also showcased along the African Diaspora Heritage Trail. This trail takes visitors on a poignant journey, highlighting the history and contributions of Africans and their descendants on the island. From the Tucker House Museum, which sheds light on the lives of enslaved Africans, to the Sally Bassett Memorial, which honors the memory of a courageous freedom fighter, these sites provide insights into Bermuda's complex past and the resilience of its people.

Exploring Bermuda's historical sites and museums is a captivating experience that unveils the layers of the island's rich heritage. From the colonial charm of St. George to the maritime legacies at the Royal Naval Dockyard, each site offers a unique window into Bermuda's past. These cultural landmarks preserve history and foster a deeper understanding and appreciation for the island's vibrant present.

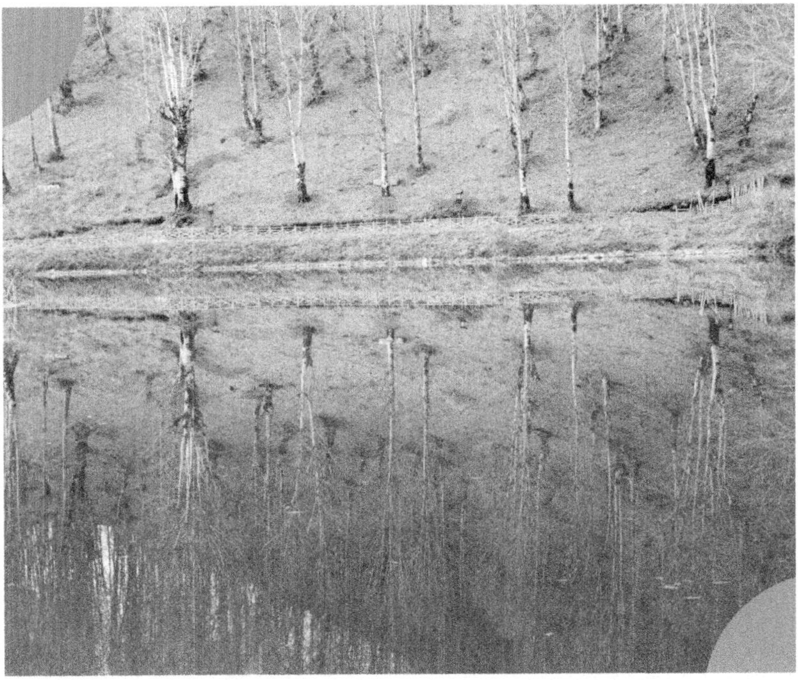

OUTDOOR ACTIVITIES

AND ADVENTURES

Bermuda, a British island territory located in the North Atlantic Ocean, is a haven for outdoor enthusiasts seeking adventure and natural beauty. The island is surrounded by crystal clear turquoise waters and boasts a mild subtropical climate, making it an ideal destination for outdoor activities and adventures. From exploring coral reefs to hiking trails, there's something for everyone in Bermuda.

One of Bermuda's most popular outdoor activities is snorkeling or scuba diving. The island's clear waters offer excellent visibility for exploring its coral reefs, shipwrecks, and diverse marine life. For those who prefer to stay above the water, there are plenty of options for sailing, kayaking, or paddleboarding around the island's many coves and bays.

Bermuda's rugged coastline and lush greenery also provide excellent opportunities for hiking and biking. Several nature reserves and parks offer well-maintained trails through forests, along cliff edges, and around scenic vistas. For those seeking a more adrenaline-fueled adventure, cliff jumping and rock climbing are also popular options.

Bermuda offers abundant outdoor activities and adventures for nature lovers and adventure seekers. With its stunning natural beauty and mild climate, it's a destination that will satisfy those looking for an active vacation.

Snorkeling and Diving

Snorkeling and diving in Bermuda offer unparalleled opportunities to explore the island's vibrant marine ecosystem and discover the hidden treasures beneath its turquoise waters. With its thriving coral reefs, diverse marine life, and numerous shipwrecks, Bermuda is a dream destination for both beginners and experienced snorkelers and divers.

Snorkeling in Bermuda is a popular activity that allows visitors to witness underwater wonders without requiring extensive training or equipment. The island has numerous snorkeling sites catering to all skill levels. From shallow, calm bays to offshore reefs, there are plenty of options to choose from.

One of the highlights of snorkeling in Bermuda is the chance to explore its magnificent coral reefs. These underwater gardens are teeming with colorful fish, intricate coral formations, and other fascinating marine creatures. Snorkelers can spot parrotfish, butterflyfish, wrasses, and even the occasional turtle or ray gliding gracefully through the clear waters.

Bermuda offers exceptional diving opportunities for those seeking a more immersive underwater experience. The island is surrounded by vast shipwrecks, which have become artificial reefs over the years. These wrecks, ranging from shallow to deep depths, attract divers worldwide.

One of the most famous wrecks is the HMS Vixen, located near Bermuda's western coastline. This British warship sank in 1896 and now lies in relatively shallow waters, making it accessible to both snorkelers and divers. The shipwreck is adorned with corals and serves as a habitat for various marine species, providing a unique and captivating dive experience.

Another notable wreck is the Cristobal Colon, a massive Spanish luxury liner that sank in 1936. Resting at depths ranging from 18 to 24 meters (60 to 80 feet), this shipwreck offers an exhilarating dive for advanced divers. The wreck is beautifully preserved, and divers can explore its impressive structure and encounter schools of fish that have made it their home.

Bermuda's crystal-clear waters, warm temperatures, and excellent visibility throughout the year make it an ideal destination for snorkeling and diving. Whether you are a beginner or an experienced diver, the underwater world of Bermuda promises an unforgettable adventure filled with awe-inspiring marine life and intriguing shipwrecks.

Sailing and Boating

Sailing and boating in Bermuda offer a remarkable way to experience the beauty of the island and its surrounding waters. With its favorable wind conditions, stunning coastline, and abundant marine life, Bermuda is a paradise for sailing enthusiasts and boaters alike.

Bermuda's location in the North Atlantic Ocean provides a perfect setting for sailing. The island is known for its consistent trade winds, which make for excellent sailing conditions throughout the year. These steady breezes and the island's clear, turquoise waters create an idyllic environment for sailors to explore the coastline and enjoy the thrill of gliding across the waves.

One of the highlights of sailing in Bermuda is participating in or witnessing world-class sailing events. The island has a rich sailing heritage and is renowned for hosting prestigious regattas like the America's Cup. The America's Cup, the oldest trophy in international sport, was held in Bermuda in 2017, attracting top sailors from around the globe. Sailing enthusiasts can also witness local races and events that showcase the island's strong sailing culture.

Boating in Bermuda offers a diverse range of options for those who prefer a more leisurely experience on the water. Visitors can rent boats, yachts, or catamarans to explore the island's picturesque coastline at their own pace. The tranquil bays, secluded coves, and hidden beaches make for perfect destinations to drop anchor and enjoy a day of relaxation and swimming.

The waters surrounding Bermuda are also popular with fishing enthusiasts. The island's deep-sea fishing charters offer thrilling opportunities to catch prized game fish, such as marlin, wahoo, and tuna. Whether you are an experienced angler or a novice fisherman, Bermuda's waters provide abundant opportunities for a rewarding fishing experience.

Safety is a priority in Bermuda's waters, and visitors are encouraged to familiarize themselves with local boating regulations and navigational guidelines. The island's marinas and yacht clubs offer services and amenities to cater to the needs of sailors and boaters, including moorings, fuel, and equipment rentals.

Sailing and boating in Bermuda offer a unique way to explore the island's stunning coastline, enjoy the thrill of the open water, and discover the wealth of marine life that surrounds the island. Whether you choose to sail competitively, charter a boat for a leisurely day on the water, or try your hand at fishing, Bermuda's waters provide a memorable and fulfilling experience for all.

Golfing in Bermuda

Golfing in Bermuda is a true delight for enthusiasts of the sport. With its lush green fairways, stunning ocean views, and world-class golf courses, the island offers a remarkable golfing experience that is hard to match.

Bermuda is home to several top-notch golf courses designed by renowned architects. These courses provide challenging gameplay and showcase the island's natural beauty. One of the most famous courses is the Port Royal Golf Course, which has hosted the PGA Grand Slam of Golf. This championship course offers breathtaking panoramic views of the Atlantic Ocean. It features undulating fairways and challenging bunkers, making it a favorite among golfers.

Mid Ocean Club is another gem on the island, designed by renowned architect Charles Blair Macdonald. This classic course features strategic bunkering, narrow fairways, and beautiful ocean vistas, providing a challenging yet scenic round of golf. The course has attracted golfers from around the world and has hosted prestigious events, including the PGA Tour.

For those seeking a more relaxed golfing experience, Bermuda offers a variety of courses suitable for all skill levels. Belmont Hills Golf Club, located in Warwick Parish, is a picturesque 18-hole course set amid rolling hills and stunning water views. This course combines a mix of challenging holes and picturesque scenery, providing an enjoyable and rewarding golfing experience.

Bermuda's temperate climate allows for year-round golfing, making it an ideal destination for golfers seeking to escape colder climates during the winter months. The island's well-maintained courses, natural beauty, and ocean views create an unforgettable golfing experience.

Beyond the golf courses, Bermuda offers excellent amenities for golfers. The island is home to world-class resorts and hotels that cater to golf enthusiasts, offering packages that include accommodations, access to golf courses, and additional amenities. These establishments provide a luxurious and convenient experience for golfers, ensuring a memorable stay on the island.

Golfing in Bermuda provides a unique blend of challenging gameplay, stunning landscapes, and world-class amenities. From championship courses with breathtaking ocean views to more relaxed options suitable for all skill levels, the island offers a golfing experience that is sure to impress. Whether you are a passionate golfer or a casual player, Bermuda's golf courses are a must-visit destination for anyone looking to enjoy the sport in a picturesque setting.

Hiking and Nature Trails

While Bermuda is known for its stunning beaches and turquoise waters, the island also boasts an array of scenic hiking trails and nature reserves that allow visitors to immerse themselves in its lush landscapes and diverse ecosystems. From coastal cliffs to dense forests, these trails offer a unique opportunity to explore Bermuda's natural beauty and discover hidden gems off the beaten path.

One popular hiking destination is the Railway Trail, a historic path that follows the route of Bermuda's former railway system. Stretching for over 18 miles, the trail meanders through picturesque landscapes, providing breathtaking views of the coastline, verdant hillsides, and charming villages. Hikers can explore sections of the trail at their own pace, enjoying the tranquility of nature and the gentle ocean breeze.

For those seeking a more adventurous hiking experience, Cooper's Island Nature Reserve is a must-visit. Located on the island's southeastern tip, this reserve boasts a network of trails that wind through coastal habitats, salt marshes, and rocky shores. Visitors hiking along the trails can spot various wildlife, including migratory birds, turtles, and native flora. The panoramic views of the Atlantic Ocean and the rugged cliffs make it a truly memorable hiking destination.

Another notable hiking trail is the Blue Hole Park in Hamilton Parish. This scenic nature reserve features a series of interconnected trails that lead to mesmerizing turquoise sinkholes, lush vegetation, and serene ponds. The trail system offers a range of difficulty levels, making it accessible to hikers of various fitness levels. Nature enthusiasts will appreciate the opportunity to observe native plant species and spot endemic birds while exploring the park's hidden corners.

For a glimpse into Bermuda's diverse flora and fauna, Spittal Pond Nature Reserve in Smith's Parish is a fantastic choice. This expansive reserve encompasses coastal areas, woodlands, and wetlands, providing a haven for wildlife. Hikers can follow the trails that meander through the reserve, taking in the breathtaking views and encountering native and migratory birds along the way.

As with any outdoor activity, hikers must be prepared and mindful of their surroundings. Wearing proper footwear, carrying water and sunscreen, and adhering to trail rules and regulations are essential for a safe and enjoyable experience.

Bermuda's hiking and nature trails offer a chance to connect with the island's natural wonders and appreciate its unspoiled landscapes. Whether you're seeking a leisurely stroll or a more challenging hike, these trails provide an escape from the ordinary, allowing visitors to embrace Bermuda's abundant natural beauty and create lasting memories.

Fishing and Deep-Sea Excursions

With its crystal-clear waters and rich marine life, Bermuda is a paradise for fishing enthusiasts and adventure seekers alike. Whether you're a seasoned angler or a novice looking for a memorable experience, the island offers a range of fishing and deep-sea excursions that promise exhilarating moments and the chance to reel in a prized catch.

Bermuda's waters are teeming with a variety of fish species, including marlin, tuna, wahoo, and snapper, making it a prime destination for sport fishing. Numerous charter companies and experienced guides are available to help visitors navigate the waters and increase their chances of a successful fishing trip. From half-day excursions to full-day adventures, fishing charters cater to all levels of expertise and provide all the necessary equipment, ensuring a hassle-free experience.

Deep-sea excursions offer the opportunity to venture beyond the shoreline and explore the vast expanse of the Atlantic Ocean surrounding Bermuda. These excursions take participants to the edge of the continental shelf, where the waters are known for their abundance of game fish. Whether trolling for big game species or bottom fishing for reef fish, deep-sea excursions provide an unforgettable adventure as you cast your lines into the deep blue depths.

Bermuda is particularly renowned for its sport fishing tournaments, attracting anglers from around the world. These tournaments offer a chance to compete for prestigious titles and showcase fishing skills while enjoying the camaraderie of fellow enthusiasts. The events are thrilling for participants and create an electric atmosphere for spectators, with weigh-ins, prize ceremonies, and festive gatherings.

Shore fishing is a popular option for those who prefer a more leisurely fishing experience. The island offers numerous spots where anglers can cast their lines from the shoreline and enjoy the tranquility of the coastal environment. From secluded coves to rocky outcrops, the diverse shoreline of Bermuda provides ample opportunities for a relaxing day of fishing.

It's important to note that fishing in Bermuda is regulated to ensure the sustainability of marine resources. Some fish species have specific sizes and catch limits, and certain areas may be protected as marine reserves. Familiarizing yourself with local fishing regulations and guidelines to promote responsible and sustainable fishing practices is essential.

Fishing and deep-sea excursions in Bermuda are more than just a hobby; they are an opportunity to connect with the island's vibrant marine ecosystem and experience the thrill of reeling in a prized catch. Whether you're a seasoned angler or a first-time fisherman, these excursions offer unforgettable moments on the open waters, surrounded by Bermuda's natural beauty and the excitement of the chase.

Cave Explorations

Bermuda's captivating beauty extends far beyond its pristine beaches and turquoise waters. The island is also home to a mesmerizing underground world of caves and caverns, offering adventurous visitors a unique and thrilling experience. Exploring these natural wonders unveils a hidden realm filled with geological formations, crystal-clear pools, and ancient stalactites and stalagmites.

Crystal Caves, located in Hamilton Parish, is one of Bermuda's most renowned cave systems. As you descend into the depths of the cave, you'll be awestruck by the ethereal beauty of the crystalline stalactites and stalagmites formed over millions of years. The shimmering underground lake, known as the "Crystal Lake," adds to the magical ambiance of the cave. Guided tours provide fascinating insights into the formation of these caves and their geological significance, allowing visitors to appreciate the intricate beauty of nature's handiwork.

Fantasy Cave, also located in Hamilton Parish, offers another enchanting underground adventure. This cave system boasts stunning formations and intricate calcite mineral deposits. As you wander through the caverns, your imagination will run wild, as the cave's unique lighting highlights the natural formations, creating an otherworldly atmosphere. The knowledgeable guides share captivating stories and folklore associated with the caves, adding to the sense of wonder.

Bermuda's caves are not limited to just the two well-known systems. The island is speckled with smaller, lesser-known caves waiting to be explored. Some caves, such as Admiralty Cave and Cathedral Cave, can be found along the coastline, accessible via rugged trails and stairs. These coastal caves offer picturesque ocean views and provide a unique perspective of Bermuda's natural beauty.

While cave exploration is an exciting adventure, it's important to prioritize safety. Guided tours are highly recommended, as experienced cave guides ensure visitors' well-being and provide valuable insights into the cave's history and geological features. Additionally, proper footwear, adequate lighting, and caution while navigating the cave's uneven terrain is essential for a safe and enjoyable experience.

Bermuda's caves offer a captivating journey into the island's geological past, allowing visitors to witness the intricate wonders hidden beneath the surface. From the mesmerizing formations of Crystal Caves to the mystical ambiance of Fantasy Cave, each cave presents a unique opportunity to explore and appreciate the island's natural treasures. Embarking on cave exploration in Bermuda is a truly unforgettable experience that unveils a world of beauty and mystery.

Whale Watching

Bermuda's azure waters are not only a haven for marine life but also offer a thrilling opportunity to witness the majestic giants of the ocean – whales. From humpback whales to pilot whales, these magnificent creatures migrate through the waters of Bermuda, captivating visitors with their awe-inspiring displays and graceful movements.

One of the best times to embark on a whale-watching adventure in Bermuda is during the winter months, from December to March. During this period, humpback whales make their annual migration from the cold Arctic waters to the warmer waters of the Caribbean. Bermuda serves as a crucial resting and breeding ground for these incredible mammals, providing a unique opportunity to observe their behaviors up close.

Several local operators offer whale-watching tours that take visitors out to the open waters to encounter these majestic creatures. Expert guides provide fascinating insights into the whales' behaviors, migration patterns, and conservation efforts. They are well-versed in locating and interpreting the whales' movements, ensuring an enriching and memorable experience.

The most common species encountered during whale-watching tours in Bermuda are humpback whales and pilot whales. Humpbacks are known for their impressive acrobatic displays, breaching, tail slapping, and even singing. Witnessing these gentle giants leaping out of the water or slapping their tails against the surface is a truly remarkable sight. On the other hand, pilot whales are known for their tight-knit social groups and sleek appearances. They often travel in pods, providing an opportunity to observe their social interactions and synchronized swimming.

Whale-watching tours not only offer the chance to witness these incredible marine mammals but also contribute to ongoing conservation efforts. By supporting responsible operators, visitors can help promote sustainable practices and raise awareness about the importance of preserving the marine environment and protecting whale populations.

It's important to remember that whale-watching is a nature-based activity that requires patience and respect for the animals. Whales are wild creatures, and their behavior can be unpredictable. The guidelines and regulations provided by tour operators should be followed to ensure the safety of both the visitors and the whales.

Embarking on a whale-watching excursion in Bermuda is an awe-inspiring experience that connects visitors with the natural wonders of the ocean. Witnessing the grace and power of these magnificent creatures in their natural habitat leaves a lasting impression and deepens our appreciation for the incredible diversity of marine life that calls Bermuda's waters home.

Eco-Tourism in Bermuda

With its pristine landscapes and rich biodiversity, Bermuda is an ideal destination for eco-tourism. The island's commitment to preserving its natural resources and promoting sustainable practices allows visitors to immerse themselves in the beauty of the environment while minimizing their impact on the ecosystem.

One of the key aspects of eco-tourism in Bermuda is the conservation of its marine ecosystems. The island is surrounded by vibrant coral reefs teeming with colorful fish and other marine species. Snorkeling and scuba diving excursions allow visitors to explore these underwater wonders while promoting responsible practices such as reef-safe sunscreen and avoiding contact with the fragile coral.

Bermuda's commitment to sustainable fishing practices is also evident in its eco-tourism offerings. Visitors can engage in responsible fishing charters that adhere to local regulations and promote catch-and-release practices, ensuring the long-term sustainability of fish populations. Additionally, some eco-tourism operators offer educational programs that highlight the importance of marine conservation and the role of sustainable fishing practices.

Land-based eco-tourism activities in Bermuda focus on preserving the island's natural habitats and promoting biodiversity. Guided nature walks, and hikes allow visitors to explore the island's diverse flora and fauna while learning about the importance of conservation. From coastal cliffs to lush forests, these excursions offer opportunities to observe native bird species, spot rare plant varieties, and appreciate the delicate balance of Bermuda's ecosystems.

The promotion of eco-friendly transportation is another aspect of sustainable tourism in Bermuda. The island encourages using bicycles and electric vehicles as alternatives to traditional modes of transportation, reducing carbon emissions and minimizing the environmental impact. Exploring Bermuda's scenic roads and pathways on a bike or electric vehicle not only allows visitors to enjoy the natural beauty of the island but also contributes to a greener and more sustainable tourism experience.

Local initiatives and organizations in Bermuda actively work to promote eco-tourism and educate visitors about the importance of sustainability. These efforts include beach clean-ups, conservation projects, and educational programs that raise awareness about environmental issues and inspire visitors to become stewards of the island's natural resources.

By embracing eco-tourism in Bermuda, visitors can not only experience the island's natural beauty but also contribute to its preservation for future generations. Engaging in responsible and sustainable practices ensures that the delicate ecosystems of Bermuda continue to thrive, allowing both residents and visitors to enjoy the wonders of this remarkable destination.

Festivals and Events

Bermuda is a vibrant destination that offers a rich tapestry of festivals and events throughout the year. These celebrations showcase the island's culture, heritage, and the lively spirit of its people. From music festivals to sporting events, there is always something happening in Bermuda that brings locals and visitors together in joyous celebration.

One of the most anticipated events in Bermuda is the Bermuda Day Parade, held on the last Friday in May. This colorful and lively parade features marching bands, dance troupes, floats, and cultural displays, all reflecting the island's diverse heritage. The event is a true spectacle of music, dance, and community spirit, drawing crowds from near and far to join in the festivities.

Music enthusiasts will delight in the Bermuda Festival of the Performing Arts. Held annually in January and February, this festival showcases an array of local and international talent in music, dance, and theater. From classical concerts to contemporary performances, the Bermuda Festival provides a platform for artists to showcase their skills and captivate audiences with their artistic expressions.

For sports enthusiasts, the Bermuda Marathon Weekend is a must-attend event. Held in January, this weekend-long event includes a marathon, half-marathon, and various other races, attracting participants from around the world. Runners get to experience the thrill of the race and soak in the stunning scenery of Bermuda as they traverse the island's picturesque roads and coastal paths.

The Cup Match is another highly anticipated event in Bermuda, held annually in late July or early August. This two-day cricket match between rival teams, St. George's and Somerset, is more than just a sporting event; it celebrates the island's cultural heritage. The match is accompanied by vibrant music, dancing, food stalls, and a festive atmosphere that brings the entire island together in friendly rivalry and camaraderie.

Throughout the year, Bermuda hosts various cultural festivals celebrating the island's diverse heritage. From the Bermuda Gombey Festival, showcasing the island's traditional dance and music, to the Bermuda Heroes Weekend, a celebration of Caribbean culture and carnival, these events provide a platform for locals and visitors to immerse themselves in the vibrant traditions of the island.

Whether you're seeking music, sports, cultural experiences, or simply a festive atmosphere, Bermuda offers a calendar filled with exciting festivals and events. These celebrations highlight the island's rich cultural tapestry and vibrant spirit and provide an opportunity to connect with the local community and immerse yourself in Bermuda's unique experiences.

DINING AND CUISINE IN BERMUDA

Bermuda is not only a paradise for sun-soaked beaches and stunning landscapes but also a destination that tantalizes the taste buds with its vibrant culinary scene. The island's unique blend of international influences, fresh local ingredients, and a dash of Bermudian flair create a gastronomic journey that is sure to satisfy even the most discerning palates.

Bermuda's dining options range from elegant fine dining establishments to charming local eateries, offering a diverse array of flavors and culinary experiences. The island's proximity to the sea means that seafood takes center stage on many menus, with succulent fish, lobsters, and shrimp being popular choices. Local favorites such as fish chowder, fish sandwiches, and Bermuda fish cakes showcase the island's seafood heritage.

In addition to seafood, Bermuda's cuisine incorporates influences from its Caribbean, British, and Portuguese roots. Visitors can indulge in hearty dishes like Bermudian-style codfish and potatoes, Portuguese-inspired spicy sausages known as "chouriço," and traditional British fares like beef pies and fish and chips.

Pairing these delectable dishes with a refreshing rum swizzle or the island's signature cocktail, the Dark 'n Stormy adds a delightful local touch to the dining experience. And let's not forget about the island's iconic dessert, the Bermuda rum cake, a sweet and moist confection soaked in the flavors of Bermuda's famous rum.

Bermuda also boasts a vibrant café culture, with charming coffee shops and bakeries serving up freshly brewed coffee, homemade pastries, and savory treats. It's the perfect place to start your day with a cup of coffee and a warm croissant or to relax and indulge in a sweet treat in the afternoon.

Whether you're seeking a fine dining experience with ocean views, a casual meal at a local hotspot, or a delightful taste of Bermuda's street food scene, the island's dining options have something for everyone.

Traditional Bermudian Cuisine

Bermuda's culinary scene is a delightful fusion of international influences, but it also proudly showcases its own traditional dishes that have become icons of Bermudian cuisine. These authentic flavors provide a window into the island's history, culture, and unique culinary heritage.

One of the most beloved dishes in Bermuda is fish chowder. This hearty soup is made with various fish, including local catches like rockfish and snapper. The chowder is simmered with aromatic spices, onions, tomatoes, and herbs, resulting in a rich and flavorful broth. Dark rum and Outerbridge's Original Sherry Peppers Sauce are often added for an extra kick of flavor. Fish chowder is traditionally served with a side of Gosling's Black Seal rum and Outerbridge's Sherry Peppers Sauce, allowing diners to customize the flavor to their liking.

Another staple of Bermudian cuisine is the fish sandwich. It features a fried or grilled fish fillet, typically rockfish or wahoo, sandwiched between slices of raisin bread or a soft bun. The sandwich is usually topped with tartar sauce, lettuce, tomato, and sometimes Bermuda onions, creating a mouthwatering combination of flavors and textures. The fish sandwich is a popular choice for a quick and satisfying meal, often enjoyed with a side of crispy fries.

Bermuda's Portuguese heritage is also evident in its cuisine, with dishes like Bermuda fish cakes. These savory fritters are made from salted codfish, mashed potatoes, onions, herbs, and spices. The mixture is formed into small cakes and deep-fried to a golden brown. Fish cakes are often served as appetizers or alongside other main dishes, offering a tasty introduction to Bermudian flavors.

Bermuda rum cake is a must-try dessert for those with a sweet tooth. This dense and moist cake is soaked in Bermuda's famous Gosling's Black Seal rum, infusing it with rich, boozy flavors. The cake is often studded with nuts and spices, giving it a delightful texture and aroma. It's a sweet indulgence that perfectly captures the essence of Bermuda's rum-infused culinary delights.

Exploring traditional Bermudian cuisine is a delightful journey that uncovers the island's unique flavors and culinary traditions. From the hearty fish chowder to the iconic fish sandwich and irresistible rum cake, these dishes offer a true taste of Bermuda's cultural heritage and make dining on the island an unforgettable experience.

Seafood Specialties

As an island surrounded by the crystal-clear waters of the Atlantic Ocean, it's no surprise that Bermuda boasts an impressive array of seafood specialties. From succulent fish to delectable crustaceans, the island's culinary scene celebrates the ocean's bounty in mouthwatering dishes.

Bermuda's proximity to the Gulf Stream ensures a rich diversity of fish species, making seafood a prominent feature of the local cuisine. One of the most popular seafood dishes is pan-fried rockfish, locally known as "bass." This firm and flavorful fish is often seasoned with herbs and spices, then pan-fried to perfection, resulting in a crispy exterior and tender, flaky flesh. Served alongside fresh vegetables or rice, pan-fried rockfish showcases the natural flavors of the sea.

Lobster is another prized delicacy in Bermuda, especially during the season from September to March. Grilled or steamed, the tender lobster meat is served with drawn butter or in flavorful sauces, allowing diners to savor its sweet and delicate taste. Whether enjoyed as a standalone dish or incorporated into pasta or salads, Bermuda's lobster specialties are a treat for seafood lovers.

Crab dishes are also a highlight of Bermuda's seafood scene. The island is home to delicious blue crabs and spider crabs, which are used to create flavorful crab cakes. These savory patties are made with a mixture of crab meat, breadcrumbs, herbs, and spices, then pan-fried until golden and crispy. Served with a zesty sauce or remoulade, Bermuda's crab cakes are a popular appetizer or main course option.

Conch, a large sea snail, is another seafood specialty that finds its way onto Bermuda's menus. Conch fritters are a beloved dish made by mixing chopped conch with a batter of flour, herbs, and spices, then deep-fried to a golden brown. The result is a crispy exterior and tender interior, bursting with flavors. Often served with a dipping sauce or a squeeze of lime, conch fritters offer a unique taste of the island's marine treasures.

When it comes to seafood specialties in Bermuda, freshness is key. The island's restaurants take pride in sourcing their ingredients locally, ensuring that the seafood is as fresh as can be. This commitment to quality guarantees that each dish highlights Bermuda's ocean bounty's natural flavors and textures, creating a memorable dining experience for seafood enthusiasts.

Whether you're indulging in pan-fried rockfish, savoring succulent lobster, delighting in crab cakes, or savoring the unique taste of conch fritters, Bermuda's seafood specialties invite you to embark on a culinary adventure that celebrates the island's deep connection to the sea.

International and Fusion Cuisine

While Bermuda is renowned for its traditional and seafood specialties, the island's culinary scene also embraces international and fusion cuisine, offering a diverse range of flavors and influences from around the world. Visitors to Bermuda can embark on a global culinary journey, exploring a variety of international dishes that have been skillfully infused with local ingredients and Bermudian flair.

Bermuda's vibrant international dining scene caters to various tastes and preferences. From Italian and French to Asian and Middle Eastern, there is a plethora of restaurants that showcase the diverse flavors of different cultures. Italian cuisine, for example, can be enjoyed in charming trattorias that serve authentic pasta dishes, wood-fired pizzas, and delectable tiramisu. French restaurants offer refined dining experiences, featuring classic dishes like coq au vin and bouillabaisse, paired with an extensive selection of wines.

Asian cuisine is well-represented in Bermuda, with restaurants specializing in Japanese sushi and sashimi, Thai curries and stir-fries, and Chinese dim sum. These establishments provide a taste of the Far East with their fresh ingredients, vibrant flavors, and expertly crafted dishes. Middle Eastern cuisine is also making its mark, with restaurants offering flavorful falafel, hummus, kebabs, and shawarma, bringing a taste of the Mediterranean to the island.

Bermuda's fusion restaurants take international cuisine a step further, blending different culinary traditions and techniques to create unique and innovative dishes. The fusion scene allows chefs to experiment with flavors, combining local ingredients with global inspirations. This results in tantalizing creations such as seafood ceviche with Bermudian salsa, jerk-spiced tacos with mango salsa, or curried lamb with plantain mash.

Embracing international and fusion cuisine allows visitors to Bermuda to expand their culinary horizons and discover new flavors and combinations. Whether you're craving the comfort of Italian cuisine, the exotic spices of Asia, or the bold flavors of fusion dishes, Bermuda's international dining scene offers a wide range of options to satisfy every palate.

From casual bistros to fine dining establishments, the island's international and fusion restaurants showcase Bermuda's chefs' creativity and culinary expertise. So, indulge in a culinary adventure that transcends borders and embark on a gastronomic exploration of global flavors in the enchanting setting of Bermuda.

Local Food Markets and Restaurants

Bermuda's culinary scene extends beyond its renowned restaurants and traditional dishes. The island is also home to vibrant local food markets and eateries that offer a glimpse into the heart of Bermudian culture and flavors. Exploring these hidden gems allows visitors to experience the local food culture and indulge in fresh, locally sourced ingredients.

One of the must-visit destinations for food enthusiasts is the Bermuda Farmers' Market. Held weekly in various locations across the island, this bustling market showcases an array of fresh produce, artisanal products, and homemade treats. The market is a treasure trove of local delights, from farm-fresh fruits and vegetables to locally-made jams, sauces, and baked goods. It's the perfect place to chat with local farmers, sample homemade treats, and gather ingredients for a delicious picnic or home-cooked meal.

In addition to the farmers' market, Bermuda boasts a range of local restaurants that celebrate the island's culinary heritage. These hidden gems often focus on seasonal and locally sourced ingredients, creating dishes that highlight the flavors of Bermuda. From quaint cafés and charming waterfront eateries to family-run establishments, these local restaurants offer a warm and welcoming atmosphere.

One popular dish that can be found in many local restaurants is Bermuda's famous fish sandwich. These sandwiches are prepared with fresh fish, often rockfish or wahoo, marinated in flavorful spices, and served between two slices of bread with a variety of toppings like lettuce, tomato, and tartar sauce. It's a quintessential Bermudian dish that combines the island's love for seafood and comfort food.

The local food trucks and roadside stands are not to be missed for those looking for a taste of Bermuda's street food scene. These mobile eateries serve up mouthwatering treats like fish cakes, fish chowder, barbecued ribs, and jerk chicken. It's an opportunity to savor the island's flavors on the go and immerse yourself in the local food culture.

Whether you're strolling through the farmers' market, savoring local dishes in cozy restaurants, or indulging in street food delights, exploring Bermuda's local food markets and eateries is a chance to connect with the island's culinary traditions and support local businesses. It's a journey that promises authentic flavors, warm hospitality, and a deeper understanding of Bermuda's vibrant food culture.

Fine Dining Experiences

Bermuda's culinary landscape extends to the realm of fine dining, where the island's top-notch restaurants offer exquisite experiences for discerning palates. From award-winning chefs to breathtaking settings, these establishments combine culinary artistry with impeccable service, creating memorable dining experiences that showcase Bermuda's gastronomic prowess.

Fine dining in Bermuda often features a fusion of international flavors, showcasing the best of global cuisine while incorporating locally sourced ingredients. Seafood takes center stage, with fresh catches from the surrounding waters prepared with skill and creativity. From succulent lobster to delicate scallops and richly flavored fish, these dishes highlight the pristine quality of Bermuda's seafood.

In addition to seafood, fine dining in Bermuda embraces other culinary delights, such as prime cuts of meat, seasonal produce, and artisanal ingredients. Each dish is carefully crafted, combining textures, flavors, and presentation to create a symphony of taste on the plate. From elegant tasting menus to a la carte options, the fine dining scene caters to a range of preferences and dietary restrictions.

The ambiance of fine dining establishments in Bermuda is as remarkable as the cuisine itself. Many restaurants are located in stunning waterfront settings, providing panoramic views of the turquoise sea or picturesque harbors. The elegant décor, attention to detail, and attentive service create an atmosphere of refined elegance, perfect for special occasions or indulgent evenings.

The wine and cocktail lists at these fine dining establishments are equally impressive, offering an extensive selection of local and international labels. Expert sommeliers are on hand to guide diners through the wine-pairing process, enhancing the overall dining experience.

Fine dining in Bermuda is an invitation to indulge in culinary excellence. Whether you're celebrating a milestone, enjoying a romantic evening, or simply seeking a memorable dining experience, these establishments offer a symphony of flavors, creativity, and exceptional service. From the moment you enter to the last bite, fine dining in Bermuda promises an unforgettable gastronomic journey.

Street Food and Casual Eateries

While Bermuda is known for its fine dining and traditional cuisine, the island also offers a vibrant street food and casual eatery scene. These culinary gems provide a different dining experience, where locals and visitors can immerse themselves in the island's relaxed atmosphere while savoring an array of delectable dishes.

Bermuda's street food scene is a delightful blend of international flavors and local favorites. One popular street food item is the fish sandwich, a true Bermudian classic. These hearty sandwiches feature freshly caught fish, such as wahoo or rockfish, grilled or fried to perfection and served with lettuce, tomato, tartar sauce, and other condiments. They can be found at roadside stands or local food trucks, making them a convenient and tasty option for a quick bite.

In addition to fish sandwiches, street food in Bermuda offers a variety of mouthwatering options. From jerk chicken and barbecue ribs to conch fritters and fish cakes, these flavorful treats are often prepared using local spices and ingredients. They are perfect for enjoying on the go or while exploring the island's scenic spots.

Casual eateries in Bermuda provide a laid-back atmosphere where visitors can enjoy delicious meals in a relaxed setting. These establishments range from beachside shacks to cozy cafés and waterfront bistros. They serve up a diverse range of dishes, from comforting classics to international favorites.

Local comfort food highlights casual eateries, with dishes like Bermuda fish chowder, fish and chips, and traditional Bermudian cassava pie. These hearty dishes showcase the island's culinary traditions and are often made using family recipes passed down through generations.

Bermuda's casual eateries also embrace international flavors, offering pizza, burgers, tacos, and sushi options. These establishments provide a relaxed space where visitors can enjoy familiar flavors or venture into new culinary territories.

Exploring Bermuda's street food and casual eateries is an opportunity to connect with the island's vibrant food culture and indulge in flavorful, informal dining experiences. Whether you're enjoying a fish sandwich by the beach or savoring local comfort food at a cozy café, these culinary destinations offer a taste of Bermuda's casual charm and delicious fare.

Afternoon Tea and Cocktails

Bermuda's culinary scene extends beyond its savory delights and encompasses the timeless tradition of afternoon tea and craft cocktails. These indulgent experiences offer a taste of elegance and provide the perfect opportunity to relax and savor the finer things in life while enjoying the island's beautiful surroundings.

Afternoon tea in Bermuda is a cherished tradition influenced by British heritage. It's a chance to slow down, socialize, and indulge in a delightful array of finger sandwiches, freshly baked scones with clotted cream and jam, and an assortment of pastries and cakes. Accompanied by a pot of fine tea, this refined ritual can be enjoyed in elegant tearooms, historic hotels, or charming cafes. The tranquil atmosphere and exquisite treats create a sense of sophistication and allow guests to unwind in style.

In addition to afternoon tea, Bermuda boasts a vibrant cocktail culture that is celebrated throughout the island. From classic concoctions to creative mixology, the cocktail scene offers a diverse range of libations to suit every taste. Whether you prefer a refreshing rum swizzle, a sophisticated martini, or a tropical concoction, Bermuda's skilled bartenders craft cocktails using locally sourced ingredients and international spirits. The combination of expert craftsmanship, beautiful settings, and the island's relaxed ambiance creates an unforgettable cocktail experience.

Many bars and lounges in Bermuda offer breathtaking views of the turquoise waters or charming harbor vistas, making them the perfect spot to sip on a cocktail and watch the sunset. The island's cocktail scene also extends to beachside bars and lively establishments, where live music and a vibrant atmosphere add to the enjoyment of the libations.

Afternoon tea and cocktails in Bermuda provide an escape into a world of refined flavors and relaxed elegance. Whether you're indulging in delicate tea and delectable treats or sipping on expertly crafted cocktails, these experiences offer a taste of luxury and an opportunity to create lasting memories in the enchanting setting of Bermuda.

Bermudian Rum and Beer

When it comes to alcoholic beverages, Bermuda is renowned for its exceptional rum and locally brewed beers. These libations capture the essence of the island's rich history, vibrant culture, and warm hospitality, making them an integral part of Bermuda's drinking scene.

Bermuda's rum heritage dates back centuries, with the island being a significant player in the rum trade during the colonial era. Today, Bermudian rum continues to be celebrated for its quality and distinctive flavors. Crafted with precision and care, Bermudian rum is known for its smoothness, complexity, and notes of caramel, vanilla, and tropical fruits. Whether enjoyed neat, on the rocks, or in a delicious cocktail, Bermudian rum offers a taste of the island's spirit and craftsmanship.

Bermuda is also home to a burgeoning craft beer scene, with local breweries producing a variety of flavorful and unique beers. From light and refreshing ales to robust stouts and hoppy IPAs, Bermuda's craft beers cater to a range of preferences. Brewed using the finest ingredients and innovative techniques, these beers often feature local flavors and influences, creating a distinct and memorable drinking experience.

In addition to rum and craft beer, Bermuda is known for its signature drink, the Dark 'n Stormy. This iconic cocktail combines Bermudian black rum, typically Goslings Black Seal, with ginger beer and a squeeze of fresh lime. It's a refreshing and flavorful concoction that has become synonymous with Bermuda and is enjoyed by locals and visitors alike.

Exploring the world of Bermudian rum and beer is an opportunity to discover the island's craftsmanship and celebrate its flavors. Whether you're sipping on a handcrafted cocktail, sampling a local brew, or raising a glass of Bermudian rum, these libations embody the island's spirit and contribute to a vibrant drinking culture in Bermuda. Cheers to the traditions, artistry, and hospitality that make Bermudian rum and beer truly special.

SHOPPING AND SOUVENIRS

Bermuda offers a delightful shopping experience, with various stores and boutiques catering to every taste and interest. From high-end luxury brands to local artisans and unique boutiques, the island provides ample opportunities to find special treasures and souvenirs to commemorate your time in Bermuda.

The shopping scene in Bermuda reflects the island's diverse culture and influences. Visitors can explore charming shopping districts, such as Front Street in Hamilton and Water Street in St. George's, where a mix of international brands, designer boutiques, and local shops line the streets. These areas offer a vibrant atmosphere, with bustling cafés, art galleries, and gift shops that showcase Bermuda's creativity and craftsmanship.

When it comes to souvenirs, Bermuda offers an array of unique items that capture the essence of the island. From handcrafted jewelry made with Bermuda's famous pink sand and local gemstones to beautiful pottery, artwork, and woven baskets, there are plenty of choices to find a special memento of your visit. Don't forget to explore the local craft markets and pop-up stalls, where artisans showcase their handmade creations, including Bermuda-inspired artwork, textiles, and culinary delights.

Whether you're looking for luxury goods, locally made crafts, or stylish fashion finds, shopping in Bermuda is a delightful experience that allows you to discover the island's unique treasures. From unique souvenirs to fashionable finds, Bermuda offers something for every shopper to take home a piece of the island's charm.

Bermuda's Shopping Districts

Bermuda is a shopper's paradise, offering a diverse range of shopping districts where visitors can find everything from high-end luxury goods to locally crafted treasures. Each shopping district has its own unique charm, atmosphere, and selection of stores, creating a delightful retail experience for those seeking to explore Bermuda's shopping scene.

Front Street in Hamilton is one of the island's premier shopping destinations. This vibrant street is lined with colorful storefronts, offering a mix of high-end fashion brands, designer boutiques, and specialty stores. Front Street is a shopper's dream, where you can find the latest fashion trends, fine jewelry, perfumes, and luxury goods. Additionally, there are art galleries, souvenir shops, and cafes, creating a lively atmosphere for strolling and exploring.

Water Street in St. George's is another must-visit shopping district in Bermuda. With its historical charm and picturesque setting, this quaint street offers a range of boutiques, gift shops, and art galleries. Here, you can find unique treasures such as handmade crafts, local artwork, pottery, and Bermuda-inspired souvenirs. Water Street is a wonderful place to soak up the ambiance of St. George's while discovering one-of-a-kind items to take home.

In addition to Front Street and Water Street, other shopping districts in Bermuda include the Clocktower Mall at the Royal Naval Dockyard and the Washington Mall in Hamilton. The Clocktower Mall offers a mix of shops, including clothing stores, jewelry shops, and artisanal boutiques. The Washington Mall is a popular shopping complex with multiple levels of stores, offering a wide variety of products, from fashion and accessories to electronics and cosmetics.

Exploring Bermuda's shopping districts is not only an opportunity to indulge in retail therapy but also a chance to soak up the island's unique atmosphere and discover local craftsmanship. Whether you're seeking luxury brands, locally made treasures, or a charming shopping experience, Bermuda's shopping districts provide an array of choices to cater to every taste and interest.

Local Art and Handicrafts

Bermuda is a haven for art enthusiasts and collectors, with a vibrant arts and crafts scene that showcases the island's creative spirit and cultural heritage. Local artists and artisans produce a wide range of captivating works, including paintings, sculptures, ceramics, textiles, and jewelry, all reflecting the unique beauty and character of Bermuda.

One of Bermuda's most distinctive art forms is the iconic "Bermuda Rig" sailboat model. These meticulously crafted miniature replicas of traditional Bermuda sloops are made by skilled craftsmen using techniques passed down through generations. These models' intricate details and craftsmanship make them highly sought-after souvenirs and keepsakes.

Bermuda's artistic talent extends beyond sailboat models. The island is home to numerous galleries and art studios where visitors can explore and purchase locally created artworks. From vibrant seascapes and landscapes to abstract compositions and contemporary pieces, Bermuda's art scene offers a diverse range of styles and mediums. Many artists draw inspiration from the island's natural beauty, vibrant colors, and cultural heritage, resulting in captivating works that capture the essence of Bermuda.

Handicrafts also play a significant role in Bermuda's artistic landscape. Local artisans produce unique creations such as pottery, handwoven baskets, quilts, and cedar woodwork. These traditional crafts showcase Bermuda's rich cultural heritage and craftsmanship, with many artisans incorporating traditional techniques and materials into their work.

When visiting Bermuda, art enthusiasts, and collectors can explore art galleries, craft markets, and boutiques to discover the wealth of local artistic talent. These venues often host exhibitions and events that provide an opportunity to meet the artists, learn about their creative processes, and acquire one-of-a-kind pieces directly from the makers.

By supporting local art and handicrafts in Bermuda, visitors bring home unique and meaningful pieces and contribute to preserving and promoting the island's vibrant artistic community. Whether you're a seasoned collector or simply appreciate the beauty of handmade creations, Bermuda's local art and handicrafts offer a window into the island's creative soul and cultural heritage.

Traditional Clothing and Textiles

Bermuda's traditional clothing and textiles are steeped in history and reflect the island's unique blend of cultures and influences. From the iconic Bermuda shorts to colorful madras fabrics, these elements of traditional attire have become synonymous with the island's timeless style and laid-back elegance.

One of Bermuda's most recognizable pieces of traditional clothing is the Bermuda shorts. Originating from British military attire, Bermuda shorts are tailored knee-length shorts typically worn with knee socks, a dress shirt, a blazer, and loafers. This iconic style is a staple of Bermuda's dress code and is often seen worn by locals and visitors alike. The shorts are available in various colors and fabrics, allowing individuals to express their personal style while adhering to the island's sartorial traditions.

Another distinctive feature of Bermuda's traditional clothing is the use of madras fabric. Madras is a brightly colored and plaid cotton fabric that has its roots in India. It was introduced to Bermuda by the British in the 17th century and has since become synonymous with the island's fashion. Madras is commonly used to make shirts, dresses, skirts, and accessories, infusing vibrant colors and patterns into Bermuda's traditional textile heritage.

In addition to Bermuda shorts and madras fabric, other traditional clothing items and accessories include straw hats, Bermuda bags, and handwoven baskets. Straw hats provide shade from the sun and are often adorned with ribbons and flowers, adding a touch of charm to any outfit. Bermuda bags, made from woven straw or fabric, are popular accessories that showcase the island's craftsmanship and are cherished as fashionable mementos of Bermuda.

Visitors can explore local boutiques and stores to find traditional clothing and textiles when visiting Bermuda. These items not only make for stylish wardrobe additions but also serve as reminders of the island's rich cultural heritage and unique fashion traditions.

Embracing Bermuda's traditional clothing and textiles allows visitors to immerse themselves in the island's timeless style and celebrate its vibrant cultural tapestry. Whether you choose to sport Bermuda shorts, don a Madras shirt, or accessorize with a straw hat or Bermuda bag, these elements of traditional attire add a touch of elegance and authenticity to your Bermuda experience.

Jewelry and Precious Gems

Bermuda is a treasure trove for jewelry enthusiasts, offering a dazzling array of exquisite pieces crafted with precision and showcasing the island's unique gemstones. From elegant fine jewelry to stunning bespoke designs, Bermuda's jewelry scene captivates with its artistry and attention to detail.

One of the highlights of Bermuda's jewelry industry is the island's collection of precious gemstones. Bermuda is renowned for its pink sand beaches, which get their rosy hue from tiny red marine organisms called foraminifera. These organisms produce microscopic pink shells that gradually break down and mix with the white sand, resulting in distinctive blush-colored sand. From this pink sand, jewelers in Bermuda extract and cut the rare and beautiful Bermuda pink diamonds, which are sought after for their unique color and rarity.

Beyond pink diamonds, Bermuda offers a wide range of jewelry options. Local artisans and renowned jewelers craft exquisite pieces using a variety of gemstones, including emeralds, sapphires, opals, and pearls. From statement necklaces and earrings to delicate bracelets and rings, Bermuda's jewelry designers create stunning works of art that reflect the island's natural beauty and cultural influences.

Visitors to Bermuda can explore the island's jewelry stores and boutiques to find a wide selection of designs, ranging from contemporary and modern to classic and traditional. Whether you're looking for a timeless piece to commemorate your visit or seeking a bespoke design tailored to your preferences, Bermuda's jewelry artisans are skilled at bringing visions to life and creating heirloom-quality pieces.

By indulging in Bermuda's jewelry and precious gems, you not only acquire a stunning piece of wearable art but also become part of the island's rich legacy of craftsmanship and elegance. Whether you're seeking a breathtaking engagement ring, a unique pendant, or a pair of elegant earrings, Bermuda's jewelry offerings are sure to dazzle and enchant.

Duty-Free Shopping

Bermuda is a haven for duty-free shopping, allowing visitors to indulge in a wide array of tax-free delights and find exceptional deals on luxury goods, fashion, jewelry, perfume, and more. Duty-free shopping in Bermuda provides an opportunity to enjoy significant savings while adding a touch of elegance and style to your wardrobe or collection.

One of the major advantages of duty-free shopping in Bermuda is the absence of sales tax. This means that prices for many goods, especially luxury items, are significantly lower compared to other destinations. Visitors can take advantage of these tax-free prices and enjoy a guilt-free shopping experience.

Hamilton, the capital city of Bermuda, is a prime destination for duty-free shopping. Front Street and the surrounding area boast an impressive selection of high-end boutiques, designer stores, and specialty shops, where visitors can find renowned brands and fashion-forward designs. From clothing and accessories to cosmetics and fragrances, Hamilton offers a variety of duty-free options to suit different tastes and budgets.

The Royal Naval Dockyard is another popular destination for duty-free shopping in Bermuda. The Clocktower Mall, located within the dockyard, is home to a range of stores offering a diverse selection of products, including jewelry, souvenirs, clothing, and local handicrafts. Exploring the Clocktower Mall is not only an opportunity to shop for tax-free items but also to immerse oneself in the historic atmosphere of this former naval stronghold.

When engaging in duty-free shopping in Bermuda, it's important to be aware of customs regulations and duty-free allowances for your home country. Visitors are typically allowed to bring back a certain value of goods without incurring additional duties or taxes, but these limits can vary. It's advisable to familiarize yourself with the regulations to ensure a hassle-free shopping experience.

Whether you're seeking luxury fashion, jewelry, or unique souvenirs, duty-free shopping in Bermuda offers a chance to indulge in tax-free delights and discover exceptional deals. Take advantage of the tax-free prices and explore Bermuda's vibrant shopping scene to find that perfect item that will serve as a lasting reminder of your time on the island.

Souvenir Ideas and Recommendations

Bermuda offers a wide variety of unique and locally made souvenirs that are perfect for remembering your trip to the island. From traditional handicrafts to stylish jewelry, there is something for everyone.

A pair of Bermuda shorts are a popular item to take home from Bermuda. These stylish shorts, also known as "Bermuda bags," are typically made from colorful fabrics and are a staple of the island's dress code. They make a great souvenir for both men and women.

Local art is another great souvenir option. Bermuda has a thriving art scene, with many local artists creating beautiful pieces inspired by the island's natural beauty. Look for paintings, prints, or sculptures that capture the essence of Bermuda's landscapes, flora, and fauna.

For those who love to cook, a bottle of local hot sauce or a jar of Bermuda honey is a great choice. The island's hot sauces are known for their unique blends of spices and peppers, while Bermuda honey is prized for its rich, floral flavor.

Jewelry is also a popular souvenir option in Bermuda. Many local jewelers create unique pieces inspired by the island's beaches and ocean life, using materials such as pink sand, sea glass, and shells. Look for bracelets, necklaces, or earrings that feature these elements.

Don't forget to pick up a bottle of local rum or a box of rum cake. Bermuda is known for its rum, and many local distilleries are producing high-quality spirits. Rum cake is also a popular treat on the island, with many bakeries offering their own unique twists on this classic dessert.

Overall, the key to finding the perfect souvenir in Bermuda is to look for something that is unique to the island, and that captures its essence. Whether you choose a pair of Bermuda shorts, a piece of local art, or a bottle of rum, you'll have a lasting memory of your time in this beautiful destination.

PRACTICAL TRAVEL

TIPS

Bermuda is a small island nation in the North Atlantic, known for its pink sand beaches, crystal-clear waters, and charming British colonial architecture. As a popular tourist destination, planning and preparing for your trip is essential to make the most out of your visit. Here are some practical travel tips to help you prepare for your Bermuda adventure.

First, you'll need to ensure you have all the necessary travel documents, including a valid passport and any required visas or travel permits. Next, you'll want to research the best time of year to visit Bermuda, as the weather can vary depending on the season. Additionally, you'll need to plan for transportation, as Bermuda does not allow rental cars for visitors. Instead, you can rent scooters or use public transportation, such as buses or ferries.

It's also important to be mindful of the local culture and customs, such as proper dress and etiquette, and to respect the natural environment by practicing responsible tourism. Make sure to have some Bermudian currency on hand, as not all businesses accept credit cards, and you'll want to have some cash for tips and small purchases. With these tips in mind, you'll be well-prepared to enjoy all that Bermuda has to offer.

Accommodation Options

When it comes to accommodation options in Bermuda, visitors are spoiled for choice. From luxurious resorts to charming bed and breakfasts, there is something to suit every taste and budget.

One popular choice for travelers is the wide range of luxury resorts and hotels scattered across the island. These establishments offer a range of amenities, such as private beaches, pools, spas, and world-class dining options. Many resorts boast stunning ocean views and are located near popular attractions, making it convenient to explore the island.

For those seeking a more intimate and personalized experience, Bermuda offers a variety of bed and breakfasts and guesthouses. These accommodations often have a cozy and welcoming atmosphere, with friendly hosts who can provide insider tips and recommendations. Bed and breakfasts can be found in historic buildings, cottages, or private homes, adding to the charm and authenticity of your stay.

Another option is renting a private vacation home or villa. Bermuda has a range of rental properties available, from beachfront villas to secluded cottages. Renting a home allows for more privacy and flexibility, especially for families or larger groups. It also offers the opportunity to live like a local and experience Bermuda at your own pace.

For budget-conscious travelers, there are also affordable hotels and guesthouses available. These accommodations provide comfortable and convenient options for those looking to make the most of their trip without breaking the bank. They may be located in quieter areas of the island but still offer access to beaches, public transportation, and other amenities.

When choosing accommodation in Bermuda, it's important to consider factors such as location, amenities, and your specific travel needs. Whether you prefer luxury resorts, cozy bed and breakfasts, or affordable hotels, Bermuda's accommodation options ensure a comfortable and memorable stay on this picturesque island.

Transportation within Bermuda

Getting around Bermuda is a breeze thanks to the island's efficient and reliable transportation options. While rental cars are not available for visitors, there are several other convenient and eco-friendly ways to explore the island.

One popular mode of transportation in Bermuda is the public bus system. The pink and blue buses cover most of the island, offering an affordable and scenic way to travel. The bus routes connect major attractions, towns, and beaches, allowing you to navigate and explore the island at your own pace easily. Bus passes can be purchased for unlimited travel, making it a cost-effective option for those planning to use public transportation frequently.

Another great way to get around Bermuda is by ferry. The island has a comprehensive ferry network that operates between various ports, including Hamilton, St. George's, and the Royal Naval Dockyard. Ferry rides offer picturesque views of the coastline and provide a refreshing alternative to land-based transportation. It's a great option for visiting different parishes and exploring Bermuda's beautiful harbors.

For a more adventurous and flexible experience, consider renting a scooter or a pedal bike. Scooters are a popular choice among tourists as they allow you to easily navigate the island's winding roads and discover hidden gems. Pedal bikes are a slower but equally enjoyable option, allowing you to explore at a leisurely pace while enjoying the scenic landscapes.

Taxis are also readily available in Bermuda, providing a convenient and comfortable mode of transportation. Taxis are metered, and rates are regulated by the government, ensuring transparency and fair pricing.

Bermuda's compact size makes it ideal for walking and cycling, particularly in areas with pedestrian-friendly paths. Many attractions, restaurants, and shops are within walking distance of each other, allowing you to explore at your own pace and immerse yourself in the island's charm.

With its well-connected transportation options, getting around Bermuda is easy and convenient. Whether you choose to explore by bus, ferry, scooter, or on foot, you'll have no trouble navigating the island and enjoying all that it has to offer.

Currency and Banking

The official currency of Bermuda is the Bermudian dollar (BMD). The Bermudian dollar is pegged to the US dollar at a fixed exchange rate, meaning both currencies are used interchangeably on the island. US dollars are widely accepted in Bermuda, and many businesses and establishments will display prices in both US dollars and Bermudian dollars.

Regarding banking in Bermuda, visitors will find various options available. Major international banks, such as HSBC, Butterfield Bank, and Clarien Bank, have branches in Bermuda and offer a variety of banking services. ATMs are also widely available throughout the island, allowing visitors to withdraw cash in either US dollars or Bermudian dollars.

Credit cards, including Visa, Mastercard, and American Express, are widely accepted in Bermuda. It's a convenient and secure method of payment, accepted at most hotels, restaurants, shops, and attractions. However, carrying some cash for smaller establishments that may not accept cards or have minimum purchase requirements is always a good idea.

When it comes to currency exchange, it's important to note that US dollars and Bermudian dollars are equivalent in value, so there is no need to exchange currency if you already have US dollars. However, if you are carrying a different currency, you can exchange it for Bermudian dollars at banks or currency exchange offices, although exchange rates may vary.

Overall, banking and currency in Bermuda are straightforward and convenient. Whether you choose to use US dollars or Bermudian dollars, you'll have no trouble accessing banking services, withdrawing cash from ATMs, and using credit cards for your transactions during your visit to the island.

Language and Communication

English is the official language of Bermuda, making communication easy for English-speaking visitors. The Bermudian accent may have some unique variations and expressions, but overall, the language spoken in Bermuda is similar to British English or American English.

Being a popular tourist destination, most Bermudians are fluent in English and are accustomed to interacting with visitors from around the world. This makes it easy to navigate the island, ask for directions, and engage in conversations with locals.

In addition to English, some Bermudians also speak a dialect called "Bermudian English." This dialect incorporates elements of British English, African languages, and West Indian influences. While you may come across this dialect in informal settings or local conversations, you will have no trouble communicating in standard English.

Bermuda has a well-developed telecommunications network, allowing visitors to stay connected. Mobile phone coverage is generally reliable throughout the island, and international roaming services are available for most carriers. Alternatively, you can also purchase local SIM cards for your unlocked phone at various locations on the island.

Internet access is widely available in Bermuda, with many hotels, cafes, and public spaces offering free Wi-Fi. This allows visitors to stay connected, check emails, and access online resources while exploring the island.

Overall, language and communication in Bermuda pose no significant barriers for English-speaking visitors. Whether you're seeking assistance, engaging in conversations, or accessing online services, English will be the primary mode of communication, ensuring a smooth and enjoyable experience during your time in Bermuda.

Health and Safety

Bermuda is known for its safety and is considered a relatively low-risk destination for travelers. However, it's always important to prioritize your health and safety while visiting any new place. Here are some key points to keep in mind regarding health and safety in Bermuda.

Firstly, Bermuda has high-quality healthcare facilities and medical services. The island has a modern hospital, the King Edward VII Memorial Hospital, which provides a wide range of medical care. It's recommended to have travel insurance that covers any medical expenses in case of emergencies.

Bermuda has a safe and clean water supply, so it is generally safe to drink tap water. However, if you prefer, bottled water is readily available throughout the island.

When it comes to safety, Bermuda has a low crime rate, but it's always wise to take standard precautions. Keep an eye on your belongings, especially in crowded areas or tourist spots, and avoid displaying valuable items openly. It's also recommended to stay in well-lit areas at night and use reputable transportation options.

In terms of outdoor activities, be mindful of the sun. Bermuda has a subtropical climate, and the sun can be intense. Protect yourself with sunscreen, hats, and sunglasses, and stay hydrated.

Additionally, it's important to adhere to safety guidelines when engaging in water activities such as swimming, snorkeling, or boating. Follow local regulations, be aware of currents and tides, and consider using appropriate safety equipment.

Overall, Bermuda is a safe and healthy destination. By practicing common sense, staying aware of your surroundings, and taking necessary precautions, you can enjoy a safe and enjoyable experience during your visit to this beautiful island.

Customs and Etiquette

Bermuda has a rich cultural heritage and a set of customs and etiquette that visitors should be aware of to ensure a respectful and enjoyable experience on the island. Here are some key customs and etiquette tips to keep in mind when visiting Bermuda:

- **Politeness and Courtesy:** Bermudians are known for their friendly and polite nature. It is customary to greet people with a smile and a friendly "hello" or "good morning." Saying "please" and "thank you" is also important in daily interactions.
- **Dress Code:** Bermuda has a conservative dress code, especially in more formal settings. When visiting religious sites, government buildings, or upscale restaurants, it is advisable to dress modestly and avoid wearing beach attire or revealing clothing. Beachwear is appropriate only at the beach or poolside.
- **Punctuality:** Being punctual is highly valued in Bermudian culture. Whether attending a meeting, a social gathering, or catching public transportation, arriving on time or a few minutes early is considered respectful.
- **Respect for the Environment:** Bermuda takes pride in its pristine natural environment. Visitors are encouraged to respect the island's natural beauty by not littering, staying on designated hiking trails, and avoiding damage to coral reefs and marine life when snorkeling or diving.

- **Tipping:** Tipping is customary in Bermuda. In restaurants, it is customary to tip around 15-20% of the bill, depending on the level of service. Additionally, it is common to tip taxi drivers, hotel staff, and tour guides for their services.
- **Beach Etiquette:** Bermuda's beaches are a popular attraction. When visiting the beaches, respecting other beachgoers' privacy and personal space is important. Loud music, excessive littering, and public nudity are unacceptable on Bermuda's beaches.

By observing these customs and practicing respectful behavior, you will create a positive impression and have a more enjoyable experience while interacting with locals and immersing yourself in the unique culture of Bermuda.

Tipping and Service Charges

Tipping and service charges are customary in Bermuda, and it is important to be aware of the local practices to ensure that you show appreciation for good service. Here are some key points to know about tipping and service charges in Bermuda:

- **Restaurants:** Most restaurants in Bermuda will add a service charge, typically around 15% to 17.5%, to the bill. This service charge is often referred to as a "gratuity" or "service fee." It is important to check the bill to see if a service charge has been included. If the service charge has not been added, it is customary to leave a tip of 15% to 20% of the total bill amount, depending on the level of service provided.
- **Bars and Cafes:** In bars and cafes, it is customary to leave a small tip for table service or if the bartender has provided exceptional service. You can round up the bill or leave a few dollars as a token of appreciation.
- **Hotel Staff:** It is customary to tip hotel staff for their services. This includes porters who assist with luggage, housekeeping staff, and concierge services. The amount can vary depending on the level of service and the type of hotel, but a guideline is to leave a few dollars per day for housekeeping and a few dollars per bag for porters.

- ❖ **Taxis:** Tipping taxi drivers in Bermuda is customary. It is common to round up the fare or add an additional 10% as a tip.
- ❖ **Other Services:** For services such as tour guides, spa services, and hairdressers, it is customary to leave a tip of 10% to 15% of the service cost as a gesture of appreciation.

It is important to note that some restaurants and establishments may automatically include the gratuity or service charge in the bill. Always check the bill to see if a service charge has been added before leaving an additional tip.

By following these tipping guidelines, you can show your appreciation for good service and ensure that you respect the local customs regarding tipping in Bermuda.

Travel Insurance and Documentation

When planning a trip to Bermuda, it's essential to consider travel insurance and ensure you have the necessary documentation for a smooth and worry-free journey. Here are some key points to keep in mind:

- **Travel Insurance:** It is highly recommended to have travel insurance that provides coverage for medical emergencies, trip cancellation or interruption, lost luggage, and other unforeseen events. Medical care in Bermuda can be expensive, so having comprehensive travel insurance will give you peace of mind and financial protection in case of any unexpected circumstances.
- **Valid Passport:** Ensure that your passport is valid for at least six months beyond your planned departure date from Bermuda. This requirement is applicable to most international travelers. If you need to renew your passport, it's advisable to do so well in advance of your trip.
- **Visa Requirements:** Check the visa requirements for your nationality before traveling to Bermuda. Depending on your country of origin, you may be required to obtain a visa before arrival. Citizens of many countries, including the United States, Canada, the United

Kingdom, and European Union member states, do not require a visa for short-term stays in Bermuda.
- **Entry Documentation:** On arrival in Bermuda, you will need to complete an immigration form and present it, along with your passport, to the immigration officer. Keep a copy of this form, as it may be required for your departure.
- **COVID-19 Requirements:** Due to the ongoing COVID-19 pandemic, additional travel documentation and requirements may be in place. Stay updated on the latest travel advisories and ensure compliance with any testing, vaccination, or quarantine requirements imposed by the Bermudian government or your home country.

It's important to review your specific insurance needs and travel documentation requirements well in advance of your trip to Bermuda. Being prepared with the necessary documentation and having appropriate travel insurance coverage will help ensure a stress-free and enjoyable journey to this beautiful island destination.

Useful Phrases and Vocabulary

While English is the official language of Bermuda, you may come across some unique words, phrases, and pronunciations that are distinct to the island. Here are some useful phrases and vocabulary to familiarize yourself with when visiting Bermuda:

1) "Morning/Good Morning" - A common greeting used throughout the day, similar to "hello."
2) "Wha Gwan?" - This phrase is a Bermudian way of asking, "What's going on?" or "How are you?"
3) "The Rock" - Refers to Bermuda, as the island is often referred to as "The Rock."
4) "Bermudaful" - A term used to describe something beautiful or pleasing, combining "Bermuda" and "beautiful."
5) "Swizzle" - The Bermuda national drink, a cocktail made with rum and various fruit juices.
6) "Fish Chowder" - A popular traditional Bermudian dish, a flavorful fish-based soup.
7) "Bermuda Onion" - A type of sweet onion that is locally grown and widely used in Bermudian cuisine.
8) "Ferry" - Refers to the public transportation system of boats that connect various parts of the island.
9) "Moped" - A common mode of transportation in Bermuda, referring to a small motorized scooter.

10) "Gombey" - The traditional Bermudian dance and colorful costume worn during festive events and parades.

Remember to speak clearly and politely, and don't hesitate to ask for clarification if you come across any unfamiliar words or phrases. Bermudians are generally friendly and helpful, and they will appreciate your interest in their unique language and culture.

SUSTAINABLE TOURISM

PRACTICES

Sustainable tourism has become increasingly important in recent years, with travelers seeking to minimize their impact on the environment and support local communities. Bermuda, with its stunning natural beauty and unique culture, is responsible for promoting sustainable tourism practices. Here are five key sustainable tourism practices in Bermuda:

1. **Choose eco-friendly accommodations**

Opt for accommodations that prioritize sustainability. Look for hotels and resorts that have implemented initiatives such as energy and water conservation, waste reduction, and the use of renewable energy sources. Many eco-lodges and boutique hotels in Bermuda have made significant efforts to minimize their environmental impact.

2. Engage in environmentally-friendly activities

Take part in activities promoting conservation and environmental respect. Explore nature reserves, engage in beach cleanups, and participate in eco-tours that educate travelers about local conservation efforts. By actively engaging in these activities, you can contribute to preserving Bermuda's natural beauty and ecosystem.

3. Support local businesses

Choose to dine at local restaurants and purchase souvenirs from local artisans. This supports the local economy and cultural heritage. Look for establishments that prioritize locally sourced ingredients and products, as this reduces the carbon footprint associated with transportation and packaging.

4. Respect local culture and environment

Familiarize yourself with local regulations and guidelines, and ensure that you follow them. For example, taking seashells or coral from Bermuda's beaches is illegal, as they are vital components of the marine ecosystem. Be mindful of your water and energy consumption, and make an effort to reduce waste.

5. Educate yourself and spread awareness

- Learn about Bermuda's unique environment, culture, and sustainability efforts.
- Educate yourself about the importance of conservation and responsible tourism practices.
- Share your knowledge with fellow travelers and encourage them to engage in sustainable tourism practices as well.

By spreading awareness, you can help create a positive impact and contribute to the long-term sustainability of Bermuda's tourism industry.

Sustainable tourism is crucial for preserving Bermuda's natural beauty and cultural heritage. By following these sustainable tourism practices - choosing eco-friendly accommodations, engaging in environmentally-friendly activities, supporting local businesses, respecting local culture and environment, and spreading awareness - travelers can contribute to the sustainability of Bermuda's tourism industry. Let's all work together to ensure that future generations can continue to enjoy the wonders of Bermuda for years to come.

Conclusion

The "Updated Bermuda Travel Guide" is a comprehensive resource that provides readers with all the necessary information to make their visit to Bermuda a memorable and fulfilling experience. This guide takes you on a journey through the captivating history, vibrant culture, stunning landscapes, and exciting attractions that Bermuda has to offer.

Throughout the book, I have explored the diverse regions of Bermuda, from the enchanting Hamilton Parish to the historic St. George's Parish, the serene Smith's Parish to the picturesque Devonshire Parish, and many more. Each region has its own unique charm, offering a variety of experiences for travelers to enjoy.

I have delved into the top attractions, including the world-renowned Horseshoe Bay Beach, the historic Royal Naval Dockyard, the captivating St. Peter's Church, the fascinating Bermuda Aquarium, Museum & Zoo, the breathtaking Crystal Caves, the iconic Gibbs Hill Lighthouse, the educational Bermuda Underwater Exploration Institute, the tranquil Spittal Pond Nature Reserve, the enchanting Botanical Gardens, and a multitude of historical sites and museums.

The book also covers various activities and experiences for nature enthusiasts, adventure seekers, food lovers, and culture enthusiasts. From hiking and nature trails to cave explorations, fishing, deep-sea excursions, whale watching, eco-tourism, festivals, and events, there is something for everyone to enjoy in Bermuda.

I have also provided valuable information on practical travel tips, including accommodation options, transportation within the island, currency and banking, language and communication, health and safety, as well as dining and cuisine.

Furthermore, the guide has explored the vibrant shopping scene, from the shopping districts to local art and handicrafts, traditional clothing and textiles, jewelry and precious gems, and duty-free shopping. I have also highlighted the importance of travel insurance and documentation to ensure a hassle-free journey.

By providing an up-to-date and comprehensive guide, my aim is to empower travelers to make informed decisions and maximize their enjoyment during their time in Bermuda. Whether you are a first-time visitor or a seasoned traveler, this guide serves as a valuable companion, ensuring that you make the most of your trip and create lasting memories.

Bermuda is a destination that captivates with its natural beauty, rich history, warm hospitality, and vibrant culture. With this updated travel guide in hand, you are equipped to explore the wonders of Bermuda and uncover the hidden gems that make it a truly unforgettable destination. So pack your bags, immerse yourself in the island's charm, and embark on an extraordinary journey through the enchanting paradise of Bermuda.

Ruby Shawn

Can You Do Me A Favor?

Are you one of the thousands of people who have read my book on Updated Bermuda Travel Guide? If so, I'd love to hear your thoughts! Please take a few moments to drop a review on Amazon and let me know what you think. Your opinion matters, and I'm sure your review will help others decide if this book is right for them. Thank you so much for being a part of this journey.

With sincere gratitude,

Ruby Shawn.

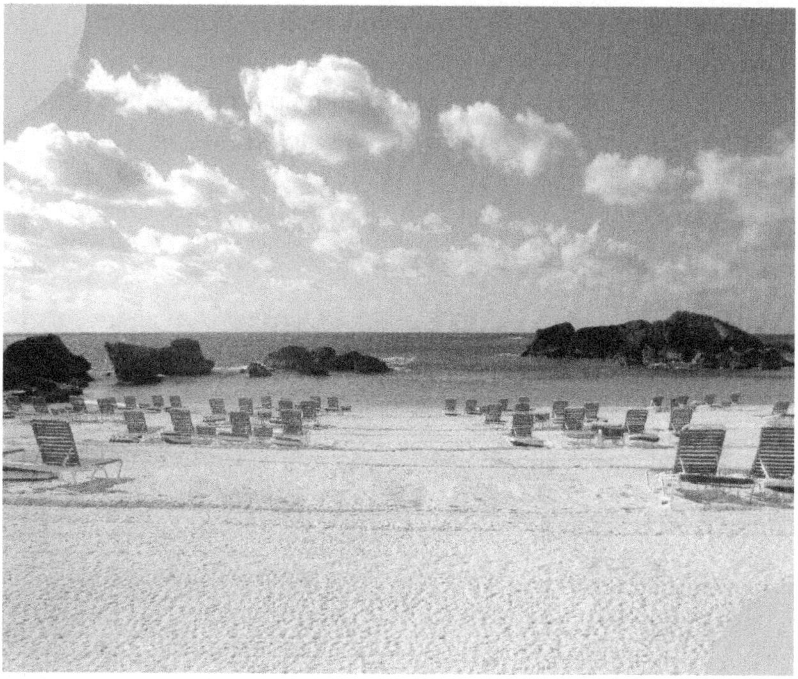